The Growing Wisdom

Red Jordan Arobateau

THE GROWING WISDOM
Copyright © 2013, by Red Jordan Arobateau
All rights reserved.

Journal #20 in the Journey Series

Any resemblance to any person living or dead is purely coincidental.

All un-attributed quotes are from the Prophet Red Jordan Arobateau.

ISBN: 978-1-304-06522-3

Published by RED JORDAN PRESS
Redjordanarobateau.com
USA

I must soon enter into a time when I am more devoted. I must look @ my art as a service to the Most High.

I must be obedient and carry my spiritual search, my devotions to The Eternal to a higher level.

Part- 1

Finally met Lonestar; hails from Tex. He lives on a trust fund of incredible monthly installments--$35,000. Yes. $35,000 *per month*—no, not $3,500 –which would be big enough, no—nearly a half million dollars per year.

He cleaned up drugs; his body looked great after stopping drugs. He had spent a lot of money on addiction.

All the money in the world can not buy the ability to get free from alcoholism or drugs, nor to sit yourself in front of an easel, or a desk and create.

$35,000 per month trust fund. I think if I had that kind of money my writing would shrink down to being a hobby.

If you hear a child who's crying, crying, crying; a dog whose barking, barking, barking; a cat screeching long & ominous—its because something is wrong.

Thus I write my JOURNEY journal.

The choir sang—he rocked & swayed as if on the deck of a big ship:

> Show the light of your Continence
> Be Merciful to us
> Your saving Hand

Men's group meeting; there the ad was, in the church bulletin.

Well you can always look at your condition as an advantage…

The OM was in angst about attending this unfamiliar group.

> Men of the Cathedral.
> Men in the community are invited to attend.

First—some were aware of his TS nature. Would some stickler be irate @ this non-male born individual's attendance? 2nd—his bad reputation amongst many he imagined, after being thrown out of one group before—and having left another because he was so offended @ how they treated him.

Evensong; here is the scripture, worthy of contemplation, especially re: his request for God, to have the gift of healing:

> And he said to them, go ye into all the world, and preach the gospel to every creature.
> S/he that believes and is baptized will be saved; but those that believe not will be damned.
> And these signs will follow those that believe; in my name they will cast out devils; they will speak with new tongues;
> Thy will take up serpents and if they drink any deadly thing, it will not hurt them; they will lay hands on the sick and they will recover.
> --St Mark 16: 15-18

Passed out a list—in memoriam—those men who have died of HIV/AIDS formerly associated to this group. As he always did, Transman looked @ the birth year of the deceased—so many born a few years younger then him, and having died years before today—made their lives significantly shorter then his own.

Been thru so much death in the gay community. Funeral after funeral—until whole barrooms were gone; 90% of gay church congregations were gone.

PM
Nada.

A beautiful passage; mystical. To match God in writing, in paints.

Friday, April 26
Am out in sun, Coyote—w/3 of older gay guys—2 of them are fighting cancer:

> We are a chemical society. In parts of Europe people live to a hundred 110. Here in America we put chemicals in the air, chemicals in the water.

Am thankful for the hot sun---

Oh in this group of gay friends who've known each other 20 years—3 of them don't like 1 in particular. If that one is there, they won't come & sit down.

2 gals walk along Polk Street hand in hand. Yeah!

Baz calls—wants to meet tonite before he goes to work @ his chauffer job.

Speak w/lady w/dog. We agreed we are seeing businesses one after another be closed down—because the rent is raised too high. Greedy landlords play w/their storefronts like a child's playblocks—gambling how high they can raise the rent—before no one will take the building, & @ that price it will sit empty forever.

> Those Chinese landlords are the worst. They squeeze; they squeeze the money.

> The Russian landlords are horrible—they are lawless.

> See this is an outrage. There is no morals left in this city.

> Its greed. Greed is king. Greed rules all.

Just heard xx killed himself. W/a gun. Young man, blond, use to sit on the side of the parklett reading. He was quiet, always sitting off away to himself—killed himself w/a gun. He was 20. One of that group of companions that sits out in alley by Coyote. Street kids.

Never would imagine all this; that the hell-terror wouldn't stop. Now there is a true horror--@ one point, 3 former friends all sit alone, along frontage of Coyote Café—in still sun, before dusk; all 3 sitting apart, non-speaking to each other any more. None of us.

Sitting in sun Olde Pervert falls asleep in the sunshine. We are getting old.

A *number* walks by—quite attractive for a middle-age gal:

> Is that a girl?

I'm not sure… yes…

Cancel.

Not interested huh.

Don't wake me up for that.

Promptly Jolly Olde falls back to sleep.

Old Man marched w/his cane again, sat in sun @ Hos.

Large curly hair dog poodle mix; horny guy, pink dick stuck out, sits panting, red tongue; tied to the fence, waiting for its owners return.

PM
I've done a helluva lot of work I'll tell you—if I'd smoked marijuana—I would not have done this much work—if I'd been a rich man's son (daughter) I wouldn't have done this much work. If I'd had a happy home, married to a woman with a few kids, I might not have done this much work. The hard-drive is sharpened by lacking things.

The desperate artistic years—you are young, fighting to maintain discipline in writing/ painting/dancing/sculpture—to have a daily routine—to force oneself to sit @ desk/easel /barre/musical instrument and not go off daydreaming, wasting your life. Later, when you have learned to overcome procrastination, writer's block etc, & work habits are etched into the marrow of your bones, you can sail thru to the end.

PPM
Horrifying news from Fukshima Dyachi. Seawater is being pumped over the fuel rods in the damaged nuclear generator #1 & 3; — continually cooling the rods keeps them from melting down—which would unleash a nuclear holocaust. However, what to do w/the used seawater—which is now contaminated w/radioactive material from being bathed over the nuclear fuel rods? For the first year or so after the near meltdown after disaster; earthquake & tsunami, which broke down the nuclear plants, this sea water had been pumped over the

rods, then held in storage tanks—because the Japanese residents refuse to let it be returned into the ocean—rightly so. But the plant officials are running out of storage space for these containers—so, they foolishly dug a in-ground reservoir to hold this radioactive sea water—lining it w/polyurethane plastic sheets & another type of sheet under that. The radioactive contaminated seawater ate thru the sheets after only 7 days and began leaking into the earth beneath the reservoir. Now the ground under the reservoir is contaminated, and radioactive particles are moving downwards into the ground water! This ground water has routes that travel deep under the soil surface using dried up riverbeds, under Japan in all directions! And on one side is heading out thru the web of dried up river-beds towards the Pacific Ocean. Now the challenge is to recapture all this contaminated water that has escaped the storage tank, plus the contaminated soil, and hold that too! Before it makes its way into the sea, and into the ground water underneath Japan. Meanwhile plans to build a plant which de-contaminates radioactive water and soil is underway, so the water can be returned to the Pacific Ocean in a benign state!

What a lot of work for a few electric lights—powered by nuclear energy! This work is costing multi-millions of dollars now, and will reach into the billions, and must be continued until some way to stabilized the fuel rods is found!

Saturday, April 27
Mailed Bancroft package off for first time. Will see when check arrives.

Came up to Coyote; saw wrestling match 3 guys—it looked serious.

Rapidly the OM marched towards Coyote—meeting Baz @ 3. Down Polk Street a great tussle between 3, then 4 men was transpiring— were they street bums? As the OM got closer he saw 3 men trying to wrestle one man down, they weren't beating him, just holding him, and w/a great exertion of strength, down he went to the alley pavement here they hold him, and the surrounding crowd of people is calling for the police on their cellphones.

GET OFF OF MY NECK! GET OFF OF MY NECK! The
apprehended man shouts.

The man had stolen 2 crystal objèct de art from the plant store down
the street, the owner chased after him, and other men joined the chase
& captured the thief.

Soon a motorcycle cop pulled up into the alley followed by 2 squads
coming from separate directions.

A blue sea of cops---one ran over to the gang on the ground, locked
the cuffs around the man's wrists and they all stood up.

Searched his pockets, his backpack

    A Chinaman! He must be on drugs!

It was a Chinese. Stocky, small; impassive face. His dirty shirt lifted
up by the cops revealed a large tattoo across the small of his back. He
looked like an ex-prisoner.

Soon the cops were taking statements from the good Samaritans who
had wrestled him down.

An idiot in the crowd of onlookers saw the items which had been
stolen and commented that it was such a fuss over those corny
things—*Just should have let him have them.* Which was truly a
stupid-ass thing to say. If a storeowner lets thieves come in and pick
out items and steal them every day they will be bankrupt before the
month is out.

What can you do w/that? The idiot commented, about the glass items.

He was probably going to run down to the TL set them on the
sidewalk and sell them—if he could get a buck apiece he'd have $2
more dollars towards a rock of crack.

One cop knelt down over the criminals backpack. There was some
green cash in it already, an envelope, which might have held drugs.

Just as the event was winding down, suddenly down on the Sutter Street intersection there is a commotion, 2 cops ran down the street, —there more hell had broken loose! 3 men fighting! They soon had a black individual in custody.

Baz has a way of saying, *I want to test something*—I.E. *I want to test the bathroom. I want to test the noodles.* To say *I want to try them and see if they are any good*—or *I'm going to test the bathroom,* meaning, I hope its in decent shape. This is funny.

PM
Interesting viewpoint from Social Anthropologist about technology companies on the forefront of invention: *We have no idea where our technology is going to go after it leaves the building.*

These giant-brain innovators don't know the social impact it will have. Recipes for revolution, disaster, mass-information, freedom? What!

They dwell in the intelligence bandwidth of raw intellect, w/out a clue as to how the world receives their products.

The weather changes so much, so fast. It was a bank of hot days, then very cold. The recent pattern is to have hours of sun, then breeze starts blowing mildly, then harder wind; the sun sets; it instantly turns cold.

> SF weather is so changeable! It's so cold!

> Don't worry it'll be hot again in another 15 minutes.

PPM
Art. It means something.

Excellent PBS program about Japanese monk; who traveled thru the land carving 20,000 statues of Buddha. In some barely unreachable caves in mountains he built shines. He was driven in his art, his meanings about nature, in his devotions.

I must soon enter into a time when I am more devoted. I must look @ my art as a service to the Most High.

11

It is odd, or, no coincidence that that most powerful vision I had @ Grace, at the Asp—was thru a religious icon, which in itself is art, painting, and Jesus portrayed in it is upholding a tablet—writing.

I must be obedient and carry my spiritual search, my devotions to The Eternal to a higher level.

I find it so compelling—the devotion—the length to which I saw, his travels to be closer to God. This mountain-climbing monk scratched his way up a steep mountain into furthest recess of a crevice to create a shrine to Buddha there.

The monk died in his 60's –strangely by the process of self-mummification—which according to the monks and doctors is extremely difficult to do. That is pretty horrible to do, not taking a very spiritual nor uplifting path @ all—this comment is according to me!

Sunday, April 28, 3PM
Just opened medical letters. Says: *you have been cut off of your medical benefits.* The 2nd page says: *your medical benefits have been reinstated.* It is all shit. Also says my foodstamp benefit will not change—what? It will be $37 per month? This is crazy shit. Must contact Rebecca (caseworker) Monday and see what it all means! This may mess up my Monday, in which I must do work online and go sit in the sun w/older gay men.

White shrieking & shrieking in her deep, heavy voice.

Church soon.

Pray; pray always.

Thru all difficulties.

Age 68. By this time the Old Man was old & full of wisdom; he exuded it, he reeked it. Also, alas, for some topics still a fool—those ornery traits.

There, they said it again: (where is this all going?) *we are still in Easter time*—when he thought Easter had come & gone! It was confusing! Hence they were reading a book on Resurrection.

Andy Loben had his priest collar neatly pinned together in back—headed class, these are some of what he said.

During prayer— *A Word for you* says the Lord.

I'll take it, Red muttered in his mind.

> God Created
> Christ Saved
> Spirit blessed the world

Human being, body, mind, are all elements of the human tangible. Accessible deeper element of who & what we are—is spirit.

There's so much more to us then just a body & the mind.

Outward and visible signs of invisible grace.

> If the hounds of heaven will peruse us we will be found.
> --Famous theologian

Now hear this—remember how earlier I mentioned a quote during Evensong, well, we discussed Mark 16. <u>It is wrong!</u>

According to Andy it is an apocryphal ending—which means it was not the original testament of Mark written 50ACE, but later written! Mark never said lay hands on and they will be healed! This is an addendum written into the bible later, by someone else! Aurrgh! And I was just about to base my whole ministry on it! (Ha ha.)

Sort of a power trip if only you personally can lay hands on and a person would be healed, what a power trip! & he (Transman) was asking to have this!

It takes us out of it—lets God alone work.

This is hard to do let the energy flow freely.

We can get out of it. W/God only.

Not a mechanistic process that automatically happens.

Step aside. You're standing in the way.

Step Aside—title of a book?

So TM was absolutely right! This was why he was @ the spiritual class! To learn! To be instructed!

Midway during this class Transman was reassured once again that we are too perfect a life—& not to end it. And that monk had died by self-mummification. *Which is horrible;* he thought. *We are not put on earth to control every aspect of our lives—including the self sacrifice of our own death—when that is usually God(ess) decision.*

> God chooses
> God bestows
> God destines
> God makes known
> God launches

Only at the end God makes known and God called us by name way before time began!

People showed their body parts to the sun all over the plaza. Arms open to greet the solar body from the middle of the labyrinth—a man opened his soul up to this vast Eternal, we know not what is the Name.

Saw an image my mind. TM's flesh teetering on a massive golden ribbon—like road— loosing my balance; he was like one of those clay statues the students make in sculpture 101 workshop—in which clay is modeled around a metal rod affixed to a wooden base—he too had a strong rod connecting him to a foundation. Its God's work and w/it he would not loose his balance, nor topple over.

The arching pillars; the great legs of grey stone columns symbolized our Mother God—a cat—Who protects Her young. The cathedral was vast. The presence of God impressed in light thru the stained glass windows in red blue green yellow.

Organ music meanders.

I am on my adventure w/Annie to unknown Chinese restaurant in SOMA district; am starving.

His stomach growling: GROWWW WWLLLLL!

First we trek to the young woman's apartment building. Very rich area Lexis, Jaguars, exclusive condos.*
 *--Apartments w/huge balconies

Quite a few Lexus's.

Just keep an open mind Annie Ho said. She told a little white fib about it being a Chinese restaurant.

This is the world of the privileged; all these teckkies from all over the globe, eat organic food, wheat grass sandwiches —made without bread—no fish, nor poultry. No meat not even meat or eggs raised humanely—thus un-empowering livestock, making cows, & chickens & pigs redundant. Firing them so to speak, so that so all barnyards would be empty. There would only be a few cows, pigs, chickens; in zoos and as memoirs in colorful picture books. Their race would dwindle from the penned multi-billions animals down to several hundreds in barnyard display parks world-wide.

There is no meat!

White, a few light skinned Latin's and a few Chinese present here, including staff; no blaxs.

Not hide or hair of tortured beef or chickens. No carnivores.

This bes a fragrance of what heaven will be like; degenerated souls called out of their suffering on this earth, to go above; and there become slender, brilliant, wise, w/whole minds; w/great gigantic genius brains.

I, and others have had visions of them in heaven. High intelligence, all slender.

They're feeling popular, free.

This has been an adventure! Exclaimed the Old Man, pleased.

Annie has been to this vegetarian restaurant for 5 days in a row and never saw the tip jar—but Red's first time there he saw that big ole tip jar with a label on it, it cries out:

TIPS!

There is a tip jar here?

I've been here very day for 2 weeks and never saw the tip jar—this is your first day here and you notice there is a tip jar!
--Annie Ho

PM

Den dey took the people who was a little bit smart, who tried to help de people—dey took dem away, then dey took the priests away.

A difficult voyage.

Monday, April 29
He went out; eyes scan the streets for foodstuffs, coins, & green folding money.

Man digging in trash, brings out can, bottle; he is w/huge parrot who sits, parked atop a trash can—2 feet tall Amazon Grey, grey blue yellow & stripes. AWWK! Deep voice. It was saying goodbye to a woman passing by who'd stopped to admire it.

I'm selling! It's a blax buyer no doubt—HO STROLL 1, 2, & VENGEANCE. Also TRANNY BIKER.

T sat in the sun basking. His hands had grown brown. He parked on
an Art Academy upscale bench. On his wei to Coyote.

Its ironic—but when in my 20's had a girlfriend who was a street
ho.—She put on one of her few dresses, tight-fitting, chose a
promising street in a commercial district and stroll down it, always
facing sideways & gazing back over her shoulder, to look men in the
face to see if she could make eye-contact. To see who she'd catch—
like a fisherperson. I think her neck had actually developed a
permanent crook in it. Now days, I'm marching down streets between
my destinations, head turning sideways back and forth gazing in the
gutters and across sidewalks up to doorways, where spare change is
often spilled.

1-silvery dime.

Oh god! Bro Blax, painter across the street is still working on those
panels! Must be 2 months now!

Old Gay Guys there for a moment. They mentioned name after name
of guys (sex trade workers) who had just gone back to the
penitentiary, or had just been released.

> They get out, then they get picked up and go right back. That's how
> they spend their lives. Going in and out of the pen.

I talked to 2 conservative people separately today out in the sun.

First, irate, was on his way to a benefit for Bradley Manning who
leaked Pentagon secrets to the press, to picket it!

> HE'S A TRAITOR!

The 2nd, a nice young bariesta from South America, who discusses the
land of Argentina, *Communism, oh that's out! No good!*

All people says the Lord. *Teach my Word to all people.*

Baz, Megan Wolfe, & I hung out for hours and had a high-ole-time. We sat in the sun @ Coyote yaking & guawaffing, until the sun shrank & disappeared. Then drove part way down to the crepe place. Delicious food & yuck yuking until the place closed. Then walking back to car, we overshot it and going back past Coyote saw some drunk had puked in the Owners flowers—yellow, lumpy vomit; not once, but in two separate locations—right on his half-barrel flower planters. Ugh. Drove on to Pirate café and talked until that closed. Then drove up to my house & sat in the white zone for passengers until the Men's Strip show theater marquee dimmed, and its door was barred.

PM
Nada.

Tuesday, April 30

He crossed the river.

Half asleep, what things crossed over his mind— what a happier place—then he fell back into the earth.

Saw Joe---looks good. Older.

We old gays all know each other—the youth recognize each other too.

3 boy toys (youth) on Polk Street, go by, they give each other the high sign. They are our pets. They know each other.

Upscale yup and a huge Asian real-estate owner confer. Business; upward climbing. Hi-end jobs. Dressed in casual clothes. Their speaking was so loud it devoured OM's train of thought:

> What I'm looking for a guy who will pay the rent, won't make a lot of noise and disturb my older tenants who're there, I've had an ongoing problem w/that.

There is no lack of people who we call losers—they are lost, yes, & few are evil persons, they were only unfortunate enough to be from broken families in the beginning, thru divorce, abuse; or afflicted by mental illness—but why can't they recover when they are offered help, time & time again?

Wealth; wealth posing in the streets in elegance; smoking cigarette, very expensive cell phone in one effete hand; cell phone robbery 1 billion a year business—I can see why. Body draped down from small shoulders; dark clothes; line of fashion; shoes are just strips of leather, bare sides, tops; this thin rich I think.

This Tuesday 7PM a horrible situation with one of the rich young yuppies are they are selfish, horrible & without compassion.

Going down the hall pulling his heavy cart of laundry; before him was a young woman sitting on the stairs—blocking them—yakking on her cellphone—blond, slender.

Coming steadily towards her turned back *EXCUSE ME!* Transman bellowed, from a distance:

> Excuse me!
>
> Could you move over? You're blocking the stairway!
>
> Why should I move!
>
> You're not suppose to be sitting on the stairway! You could be down there!

(There were 2 large abutments at the end of the stairs.)

> Why should I move, you've got a rolling cart!

–She angrily flipped her hand @ the other stair rail on the opposite side.

If truth must be told, Transman, who was disabled preferred to hang onto the railing w/his left hand and pull w/the right—the one more familiar. He was afraid he might stumble.

19

No I'm not going to move! The blond bitch energetically sprung up but did not move!

The OM stumbled over to the other side of the stairs, jerking the heavy cart, and angrily went down, unbalanced—when he got to the bottom of course the laundry tipped over.

You're going to get paid back one day but not how you'd expect it. Yelled Transman—referring to her horrible karma.

He talked to the man across the hall who commented his verdict: *no upbringing.*

The OM was drained by this brouhaha he'd had in the hall.

He spoke w/the building manager who fortuitously was walking past—who ascertained it was a young Russian woman who'd recently moved in. TM remembered the last bad encounter he'd had w/a Rooski—the one who didn't want to serve him his free coffee when the Persians owned the café, and how she'd lied about what the owner had said. And how he'd noticed how she'd sometime stare @ him, and when she observed him writing his infernal notes she got extremely agitated. He remembered how the Russian Mafia had forced all the transwoman out of a building they had purchased, and the dirty double-dealings they had pulled, in defiance of the Courts of Law in SF. Not a pleasant people it seemed, sadly.

Earlier that day he'd been speaking to the Malaysian out in the sun in front of Coyote and she'd spoken about doctors of long ago: *once they went into the profession to help people; now, its just to make money. They are running doctoring like a business.* Somebody else added that its: *all because of the GI bill. It paid for their education. Before, in the past you had to be dedicated to want to be a doctor—now anybody can be a doctor, because it's a well-paid profession.*

Saw Joe; body very trim; shorts, T-shirt, so muscular; white skin w/blue tattoos. Out in street carrying 2 backpacks w/his stuff.

The OM had known a relatively secure society as he'd grown up, 1940's, '50's—outside of the hell going on in his insane mad mother home—during his times there was relative national security. He was living safely within a fortress in one of the largest Empires earth has ever witnessed.

PM
Am in precarious position. Tomorrow is the 1st, and my food card should be @ Grace, but there is a chance it is not, since the Operative is away on Jury duty. Also, sold book last month so there should be Amazon ebook funds –however when I looked @ email on Monday, there was no indication of the funds being due—and there usually is @ this time! Called both banks, there is exactly one dollar in all 3 accounts!

The Bancroft is due in on Thursday—but has been known to arrive early—also 6 months late!

Any one of these things going into my account tonite/tomorrow AM, will save me—for I have exactly $1.50 in cash and not enough food for tomorrow. Penny Cat has her food however.

Wednesday, May 1
Don't break anything! Baz admonished. They were in the teashop of Megan Wolfe's employ.

> Very pretty. I've never had tea like this before!

Flowers on the table, flowers on the tablecloth; flowery saucers, porcelain finery, w/flower patterns; 2 saucers under a cup instead of one.

Paintings of flowers on the wall.

Lamps, padded chairs, --w/flowered chair covers…

In this place we had interesting conversations, which involved many topics including:

> There is a zealousness in religion which is negative… where one follows each law & rule to the extreme, believing this way is the True Religion, but it is not, as Jesus plainly says, we are no longer under the law, but under the Spirit. I am fortunate to have grown

21

up in my new-found Christianity in a very liberal and knowledgeable church MCC, the gay church in which scripture is analyzed and not taken word for word—which as we know has often been miss-translated. So having grown up in leap-years, I passed thru many phases as a young Christian, including the zealous obey-to-the-letter-of-the-law phase, in which, in fact, many of the ignorant churches get stuck and grow no further. So I was giving a party one nite, and had a few of my cronies assembled, and a new record player had purchased with some of my last funds. We were standing around listening to jams—Chaska Khan—I'm Every Woman--, and the doorbell rang. I opened it and to my horror saw a small Witch in black robes and blue tattoos of some demonological incantations stitched across her forehead. I was horrified! Shocked. And did not want to let her in!

What do you want!!!!

I'm here for your Halloween party!

Thank God(ess) I let her in the door. It shows how preoccupied I was during that phase of letter-of-the-law (No Witchcraft workers allowed) that kind of stuff.

PM
Nada.

Thursday, May 2
More of the privileged kids in costumes; green faces, spray-painted pink hair; march up Sutter Street.

> A gypsy curse on all trespassers!
> --Complete w/Anarchy sign on parked car
> of a homeless car-sleeper

Again look @ faces of privilege. What do they become? These richer?

> What kinds of drugs are these people on?
> --Street

See Joe packing & unpacking his backpacks.

Hung out w/Joe on Post/Sutter blazing sun.

The muscular boy toy had sketches he had done on paper w/pens.
Red congratulated him on them and said he should keep doing it.

My prayer remains.

This government is so cruel, if money comes in automatically @ end
of this same month, it will put me over the top.

& will cut me off medical benefits again!

For 2 minutes the Old Guy is really happy –then later that day he
realizes, since EFT (Bancroft) came in, in this month—May on the
1st— his next shipment might well hit @ the end of the same month
putting him over the limit—

Waiting for Dr Sam & child. Evidently when I'm not around the
child asks, *where's Red?*

This is a first-rate city –pink moustache zip cars zip around PU very
hi-end appearing folks. From moneyed families, mega skills; leaving
the poor behind; the seniors, the challenged behind; the artists. All
longing for a place in comfort and security; while these fools are
exchanging triumph stories about yuppie startups.

Re: his budget, TM had the thought he was thinking ahead but not
that far ahead. He had needed to make money—but not too much
money!

PM
Nada.

If you're doing a work of kindness, of charity, of love--you are
practically a saint; but if you are charging money for it, you are more
or less a prostitute.

This quest of greed & profit is destroying us.

Friday, May 3

Transman sat there @ his desk day-dreaming. He was trying to make happy endings out of these ugly stories of the world.

Coyote. 2 tables of transgirls in the sun---all in women's clothes, longhair; chatting in girlish voices. One utters: *WOW*, As a muscular male strides by. Laughing in high falsetto: *He is muy handsome.*

No Old Gay Men to be seen. —No Joe. Transman had the stuff for him; a found sketchbook, & found pens for his sketching.

Sun unbearably hot, but a breeze starting up.

An old lady fishes thru the trash cans. She has a pension—but not enough.

A man ambled along; he resembled Joe, but 20-years older, same prison walk slow, overly muscular, arms swinging, aimlessly @ his sides.

2 of the Old Gay Guys drove by in their cars, cruising; not enough interest in TM to stop.

Well if you have $ you have trade always. That's just how it is.

Cosmo & Joe drive by 2x's then stopped and parked down the street. The OM hoped he'd come by so he could give Joe his present. But they did not come to the café but only stayed down there @ the corner talking.

OM hoped Joe would not loose his present; he had lost so much stuff.

Giant gangly blax crow floats over, wind caught in its massive wings, intent on harassing 2 pigeons.

Spoke w/pleasant Korean.

After the Korean left, the Malaysian arrived, then here comes Olde Jolly from across the street.

T remembered when he was walking home at his childhood place @ St. Lawrence Avenue. An elder woman who lived across the street age 80's? --Collapsed & fell on the sidewalk. He saw her fall. He did not try to go over to help her but kept on walking to his house. He was almost 13. The abuse in his home had nearly vanquished him. He was emotionally dead.

Later, his grandmother in a strange, too quiet voice inquired about the incident: *Mrs. Evens fell on the sidewalk, she saw you, but said you didn't come over to help her...* And he'd only cast a strange crazy-fiendish smile of guilt, and muttered something like: *I don't know...*

PM
Nada.

Saturday, May 4
The OM woke up in increments. Life began, then retreated. Then he fully awoke, being engaged in life.

Went out today, immediately saw Mr. Wayne, on the sidewalk; -- down from the Male Strip club—posed in black clothes like a dance costume outside.

Some people there is no hope—no matter how hard you cry & pray, its not going to change.

Joe came down the street carrying 4 backpacks, & pushing a bicycle. He was w/one of his girlfriends and she carried 3 packs also.

Joe cycled down the street, backpacks jutting out behind him; cigarette smoke trailing.

The OM reached into his pack and produced the drawing book he'd found 5 years ago in Calla supermarket parking lot (Now the Ho's lot). Also a box of pens given to him by someone long ago. Joe was impressed by the gift.

Old Man sits on fire hydrant; Lexus pulls up. What a contrast.

Oh—found 1 packaged lasagna mix, & 1 red apple.

PM

Lasagna mix includes 2 fake cheeses— tasty, and the mixings for seasoned red tomato sauce.

Delicious.

Sunday, May 5,
Like a wild bitch let loose. Thar' she go!

Sleep. The sleep & awake; his departure into unconscious, wading back into deep waters, just to again awake to fit himself into the box of reality: *what day is it, what time is it? What activities do I have for today to prepare for?* Suppose to fit himself into the mechanism of human society.

The OM went out—his eyes swept the streets back/forth from curb to brick wall of apartment building for dropped coins. Today, pennies would do—needing 8¢ to round out a penny roll, and to make an even dollar out of nickels & dimes; must deposit by Monday.

Its really ironic rich yups come out here to SF, treat the City as a playland; funny they'd come into it and go home again not learning; nor seeing God's face in the destitute faces of the poor. —The poor who, by the yups very presence & sheer volume of their numbers they have helped to destroy.

An old bum come down street lit up cigarette butt—he would walk stiffly slowly right in front of the OM down street blowing clouds of blue smoke. *Oh cigarette smoke! Bad!* OM said, irately to him, voicing his rights as a citizen.

OM sat on a fire hydrant, there observe, like watching animals in a game preserve— dynastic rich who remotely only hear about poverty, —never near it. Blax wealthy are near it by 2nd hand. They po' cousins. The wealthy lost the lessons of poverty & don't care nor understand the poor.

Well we all share in the shit—those who do good, and evil-doers alike.

Sin has gone out into the world.

26

@ this point Transman needed 8¢. 2 pennies to make his 5-cent penny roll good; and a nickel to make an even dollar. He was assembling the $22.13 he needed to bring his checking account into balance.

A Chinese elder, very poor clothes, sat on a Ho's bench in parking lot; held a plastic baggie of cash--$20 bills, $10 bills, $5's and he needed 8¢! The old lady fished into the cellophane bag and folded the $20's and $10's over and over. & she was dying and so was he—slowly.

This age of fucked up kapitalism.

Down on the corner where pennies happen to roll.

The taverns jam, hypnotic beats.

YIPPEE! Screams a drunk woman. Tavern sounds of parties.

As the OM turned into the massive castlesque cathedral, which towered 8-stories above, entering thru its huge oaken doors, he stepped into a cool, somber world. Verger Elaine is lighting candles. Music swells beautifully. He has walked into an organ recital.

Last strains of music breathed out of the lungs of the organ, followed by applause from an audience scattered throughout the pews.

Spiritual Study Class.

Apocra are books written long after the scriptures. They are holy, but they are not canonized. Wisdom of Solomon. Macabees. Thomas. Gospel of Mary; are some of them. This is the technical definition. The un-technical definition is any works added on to the bible after it was canonized, which was around 200AD.

Saints started later on.

Jews didn't use the word saints. Jesus Christ gathered converts: Jewish Christians, Greek Christians, Asian Christians. Brand new Christians. To join all you had to say was: *I believe in Jesus Christ.*

They had as of yet no Nicene Creed, no vows. The new Christian churches had none of this—they might have only one book of scriptures. Someone had Mark, some had Paul.

Use of the word saint did not started until John.

According to some spiritual teachings, the measure of a saint makes it impossible for an ordinary person to attain—this is a mistake. We are all short of the Maker, we are all fallen Christians. All of us have a God-shaped hole in or souls & are aching to have it filled.

Ephesus is the only church where there is no trouble. The Galatians, the Corinthians, et all must be disciplined. Philippians, Colossians, Thessalonians. Just like the arguing, drama-fraught churches of this modern day.

God's gift is a Grace that is coming from some place other then yourself.

You have done a marvelous work of healing. Now you need to be grateful. To have gratitude—*thank you God for using me*—instead of saying, *God did it all* & thereby give God the credit and distancing yourself from it. Thank God & ask for more!

Sin; amiss of the weak, a failure to live up to ourselves into the full image of God; it's a temporary condition --we can get rid of it.

Oh did I mention the other day God showed me, indicated to me—a vision of a sketchbook & pen--& I was obedient—accepting of this vision and followed thru with it. Gratitude to God for it and invite more, many much more from the Eternal. Participate! & ask for more!

Re: the pennies—just a day before I'd passed by a scattering of pennies in the nasty gutter—and was in a hurry, so marched right by them, instead of taking the time to stoop down painfully & pluck each copper coin up w/pinch of forefinger & thumb—this is when I thought I had money, having received Bancroft funds. Now I'm 8¢ short!

Streets are empty—not a sou to be found!

TM was in the service—he sat in the pews beside the lectern—a large votive candle on a pedestal sat nearby.

He thought there was a big fat thick white flame proceeding out of the votive candle! —But when he looked over to see it was only a regular size flame.

The heat of light of the Spirit.

An iridescent green gay sissy walked by smiling; skin blax—lime green sandals, young looking, & circus yellow fingernails—ten, contrast against chocolate skin—she dazzles.

Now we all know.

Tour bus came into the church, out-of-town- tourists pouring up the steps, right at end of service—what nerve! Gawkers!

God gives visions but its up to us to realize them, and go further w/God and make materialize something not there before.

PM
Nada.

Monday, May 6
OM was weak & he realized it was from not having eaten enough late last nite—this AM. Saw a bum eating subway sandwich sitting there by the side of the road. The bum just sat there and passersby fund him w/spare change & food. It fell into his lap.

Saw Miss Daisy:

> We are going to Sac about Medical. We are going to have 12 busses,
> leaving June 4. 1 in the Fillmore, 1 in the Tenderloin, 2 from
> Chinatown, 1 in Bay View Hunter Point...
> --Miss Daisy

The Transman smiled privately to himself as he strode mightily down Sutter Street & workers looked @ him w/sour faces wondering what

29

the hell this po' OM had to smile about—Miss Daisy had invited him by bus to give his grand speech about poverty in the state capitol!

Sitting @ Coyote w/ 3 Older Gay Guys.

Saw Joe. OM bought him a soda from his humble store.

> I had food and some stuff in my pack. I set it down. Somebody took it.
> --Joe.

There is no honor among thieves. A bum will steal from another homeless man, they don't care.

One of Cosmo's trade, handsome XX greeted a woman in the street:

> She's a freighter. She hops freights. They ride the rails all over America. There are rules for riding the rails. FTR Freight Train Riders of America—they are lawless. They kill people. They kill you if they don't like your attitude.

Oh course I'd thought about it—train-hopping… back in my past, knowing it was the only thing I had not yet done. And debated if I wanted to take the risk to do that. Back then when I was in my 20's, 30's; back when flesh was burning… for adventure, for love, for the unspeakable future.

You see some walk along ragged shoes & tattered backpacks—some are crooked. Crooked humanbeings. And one such coward must have snatched Joe's bag.

PM
When the OM got his recipe for deposit, he realized his addition in his checkbook was wrong. He was still $5.99 overdrawn. His website fees came out automatically—and they were due to come in between the 6th and the 9th. He had a day to get the money and deposit it.

I had angst

The hate then the hurt.

Pain twisted out of shape.

After he'd had a dream this morning: *I'm glad not longer in racial pressure cooker as in my childhood.* Race dream.

> Back in the room where was the blax meeting, tall person, as light as me grabbed me and threw me aside!

> OM fled w/a black friend. We got off the El train @ 22nd Avenue, which was a bad area @ that time—but we escaped those racists, & I got away.

This country has engineered racism; the race between the nicest hair, the best features; battle over what skin color is better. I am different then 'my race'; I like my skin color, features, and hair are loveable to me. Battles over it, battles over what we are.

Tuesday, May 7
An old bum lay in the stairwell of dank underpass; a sarcophagus; sparse matted hair over bloody forehead & @ the other end of his blanket wrapped mummy, stuck out a pair of feet in filthy sox. Old Man stepped carefully down the cement stairs; he went around.

Movie shoot on the streets; police guarding it. The movie industry is big cash fees for the city. Trailers for costume changing & the big name stars quarters.

> I got a meaningful job for you. —A blow job.
> --Olde Pervert to passing young man

> Can you get it up?

> Yes.

> You can get it up but can you cum?

T had none of these problems.

I'll tell you I've seen people thrown away like so much garbage. I see it here, on this street.

31

Wind ruffles grey feathers of pigeon breast. Sun hot. Wind blows.

PM
There are people on this planet who got money. They did not do a thing to get this money but to sit in their cradle and go GOO GOO, COO COO! And they are given a fortune—by loving parents, and ancestors upon ancestors before them.

Must tell you interesting phenomena, am editing COLLECTED POETRY –1., it is putting me back into a time when wrote it some in my late 20's others age 15, 16.

I took risks. Made some pretty important decisions like quitting being a bum & getting job. Cleaning up tobacco, drugs, liquor.

> What is going to happen when Buddhist ideas of suffering of the East, meet the ideas of the West, of capitalism.
> --TV Buddhist

> Nirvana has no fixed point in time & place.
> --TV

Wednesday, May 8, 12-Noon
The Spirit woke me from dreams this AM, w/a Word:

Read between the lines.

Working on COLLECTED POETRY 1 before shrink apt. Am suppose to meet w/Baz, later this afternoon, and Dr. Sam tonite maybe for movie; Jurassic Park remake in 3-D.

Am now completely caught up w/bank account + $4 over, and some food stamps remaining. Am only waiting for funds to be sent! Amazon says it is sending $10 first week of *next month*, but what month is that? This one, or June?!

On doorsteps of my block found bag of delicious Asian food treat— green & yellow sticky pastry. Some French bread ends; 3 hardboiled eggs & a tamale shaped thing wrapped in string, which was rice and something yellow inside.

32

Missed out on Old Gay Men.

Saw Joel carrying only 2 bags & 1 skateboard—sans wheels.

As he & Red sat there surrounded by:

> Joes 2 bags
> Joes skateboard w/no wheels
> Reds 1bag
> Reds tote bag w/found food
> Red's cane

They shared a modest bit of the OM's food—3 eggs, and the delicious Asian sweets.

Cosmo drove up, opens back of truck & gave Joe a sack of socks and teeshirt & soda & cigarettes.

Fall in the air—makes a definite statement—warm coat needed; me, a child out @ play in the alley. Blowing frosty clouds; heading home to the house to warm up; love, hearts beating; human folk, dad and little Red. Mom growing more estranged. Mom w/her snake-like hair, and funny hidden smile.

Annie called—was so kind as to offer me left-over Chinee food, and drove me to the Ho's where got a sparkling water & meat for my refrigerator on dwindling food stamps. She drove me home and we talked awhile about her ill grandmother and her immigration status. Ah, the problems of the world.

OM problems; must live dirt cheap until after the Bancroft's fiscal year and when get my next payment from them—sometime in June. Should not dare touch the Grace monies because might need it for rent if the Bancroft comes in late! Aurrrgh!

Went to din w/Dr. Sam, discussed our mutual problems; then on to movies—Jurassic Park—in 3D! Way Fabu! And scary! The dinosaurs roaring, stepping out of the screen into our theatre seats on their 300-million year old evolutionary 3-toed feet, WOW!

PM

Have I mentioned the horrific garment workers building collapse in impoverished Bangladesh, in which over 600 people have been killed. The guards on the work shift chained the doors shut and would not let the workers leave their places on the workroom floor—even as they felt the building beginning to shake.

The owner of this greedy money-making death trap has been caught trying to flee the border into India—he was melting in the arms of the police, dragging his feet, blubbering from his mouth—in terror. He should get the death penalty. The penalty for greed!

Thursday, May 9
The Lord(ess) gave me a word awaking: *have faith.*

Blax street woman in center of the street screams out her pain. Pink handkerchief covers her nappy hair; she wreaths & gyrates, moans & screams. Dark-brown, toothless.

What great pain? What special need?

An ambulance travels down the street goes thru the green light but there she is gyrating howling in the crosswalk, it slows to a stop to avoid hitting her.

Crack dance.

It wouldn't be the richest of the richest, tho not either the poorest of the poor; they who have lost too much. They have seen too much.

Compassion.

You know the path up to the churchhouse—the Word is there, waiting for you.

Annie Ho is cleaning up her apartment, & picked up coins off the floor:

> I'll take the pennies.

> No I took them all to the machine. It was $180.

34

WHAAT!

And that's just the living room!

*This point in time.....   1 dime... never now what you might find...
you might see Jesus—or Buddha, St Mary, Mohammad... when
walking along the road.....*

So the OM walked along the road to see what he could find. Spare
change... lost people... he observed birds in flight. In the inner city
trash, debris & leaves blew in the wind.

Wow 25¢. A shiny silver coin---to add to his plastic bag of coins. Fed
birds a crust in exchange.

My God, Cosmo drove by—one piece of young trade, they meet in
the alley. Then another young guy marches by and Cosmo calls to
him from his car.

It's the youngster, Junior. Several guys have had him, they say: *He's
got a big piece of meat.*

One of the Older Gay Men spoke about Cosmo—*empty inside.* He
spoke about: *meaningful relationships.* Stuff seldom discussed down
here.

> I've seen it for the last 30 years—xxx did the same thing. Ran after
> all the cute young boys. Now he's at home in his house & don't
> trust anybody.

During the day that passed—the OM sat/w OGM (Older Gay Men) —
he saw another poor soul who'd lost his mind go running out into the
street flowing with traffic weaving dangerously between the vehicles.
What is it? Full moon? Its not the 1st or the 15th, when the GA
checks come out... maybe the crack was running good that day...

Saw a dime on street—a hustler—tripped past on her high heels PU
her due for all that fruitless walking—a thin dime off this stained
pavement; by now TM had baked brown in the sun.

She is together despite her addictions—she commands a price. She extracts a slim expensive phone from her purse; her heels are very high.

The wind is blowing.

PM
Over 600 people killed in garment manufacturing building collapse, Bangladesh. The worst industrial death toll in world history.

U$ firms largest manufacturer's there. If U$ pulls out—it will throw that nation into starvation—the garment manufacturing industry accounts for 60 percent of its economy.

I had a dream. But am not happy today. One of the worst feelings is to have said *I have a dream*—then to wake up 60 years later to know, I failed to peruse my dream; I did not catch a hold of its tail. Well I am very satisfied that I have done my dream—and am still doing it.

Friday, May 10, 12-Noon
Up AM, just realized missed my eyeglass appointment yesterday. Completely overlooked it.

Thinking about art. About painting.

According to the Buddhist teachings, man in car tried to cut me off @ intersection inside me springs up anger—hate; but this can be turned around—to compassion.

Well he doesn't know his purpose in life. I don't know but I'm on a higher* level then he is.
*--Further level.

What boy might come to him for teaching—not sex, something's can not be bought. No price in the world.

Might be subsequent sex--if we become friends.

Am thinking about the boy Hound, which is his nickname, and young Junior. 19 to 24 year old age bracket.

36

Lost piece of tooth w/enamel rotted, stained brown base—the tooth had been worked on & he'd eaten off the other side of his mouth exclusively for 2 years, per the dentist instruction but then the fascist Austrian alien elected governor had cut senior dental care and he could never afford to get a crown to protect it.

Talked to 3 OGM's—then saw C-3, artist, having show tomorrow Shotgun studio (Whitewalls), down in TL.

Sunshine briefly flashing, wind blows. Bro Leo calls, will be here then bro Baz calls will also be here in 30 minutes.

Sky grey/white flashing, classical music—piano, tinkling from inside Coyote.

Relentlessly the Owner—Gardner watered his gardens—5 gold cauldrons, 2 barrels, & 3 planters.

Sun warm.

Sun warm, life is breaking out all over maybe because its spring. Jeff (The Loin) walks by w/his baby in a stroller.

Baz may not get here—stuck on freeway—gi-normous traffic.

Baz, Monday?

T & T-Bro Leo spoke over Hebrew deli bout coming out/not coming out to new friends, and how the closer you get over time to a person, and they still do not know your T, the further separate you get—your getting closer, but as you do so the more further away you get… it pushes you apart—this secret you know but they cannot fathom.

Oh, Leo met the Jolly Olde Pervert so I told him:

> The reason why I like him is I admire anybody who has reached the age of 93—. And I admire any 93-year oldster who is still walking around, running a small business, and having sex! –Paying for it! The way we met was, he sat down next to me outside @ one of the

picnic tables in front of Coyote, somebody introduced us, and he reaches over and put his hand on my thigh and says: *I pay well.* And I politely picked up his hand, lifted it off of my thigh and carried it across the table and set it gently down on the other side of the table right in front of him and replied: *I don't think so!* So this is how we met! Ha ha ha!

Since then we've had a rollicking conversation going about the cute young men and young trade who walks past, yet sadly I'm not sure if he knows I'm T and wonder once in a while should I tell him.

PM
The young Buddha, sounds like he nearly killed himself during his spiritual seeking.

Saturday, May 11
OM made his way to Coyote. His friend Napoli bestowed a coffee on the Old Guy from out of the Persian Café redux. They chatted a short while, then on to café. All my friends busy today.

Saw small Junior—so cute.

Is he addicted? No. But he needs drugs. He lurched down the street to where the street people stay.

Hot sun—wind blew cooling it off. Seagull circled high in the sky. He looked upward, he thanked God for life.

I come to give you life & life abundant.

> Well… life… life is strange.
> Many people take it for a game.

So life goes on. People have to make some mistakes & have some regrets, naturally.

People don't have what they want in life.

The Jolly Olde Pervert cautiously, but steadily made his way across the street. They said hello— in awhile TM heard something astonishing—the Older Man exclaimed, he didn't know what he wanted in life! And he is 93 years old!

TM agreed, he too was not sure what he wanted either. He was still a seeker. *I wanted to be an artist/writer & am, I am accomplishing that, but I'm still seeking & not sure where that's going!*

Old Jolly commented when a tall man strode past:

> I like that.
>
> I don't like 'em too tall.
>
> Lay him out on the bed, one end will hang over each end of the bed. I'll start in the middle and eat towards each end.

An interesting interchange happened. Saw young Junior—he plumped down on the sidewalk, back against the wall. His greatcoat splayed out, his backpack tossed beside; his arms/legs akimbo. —We talked.

Found he, like the others is an artist. And writes. He moves around town. Here, TL, Height Street, Castro:

> If I had a lot of money I'd stay in one place too. I'd get a place and have enough dope, pussy, dick. I'd stay in one place too!

Want to have a date? I need to talk to him privately. See if he wants a date.

The kid was eager—seeing all that money in his minds eye.

Tina Turner jams over café loudspeaker—on fire, burnen' up the stage.

This street is the same as any other. Chicago, New York. The South Side. The Near North Side.

> Do you want to date?

Sure, yes!

The young man said.

Sun going down.

Waked on down the block there were once 5 coffee shops. Currently all but one are closed. Coyote is the only one open. That new café on Polk & Pine where the very nice owner hired some ex-junkie girls, and they got their sobriety & worked steadily, loyally; he might have gone belly-up. No work has been done on the place, as the weeks toll into months.

Saw a lady from church, we chat; she gives the latest report on her housing status:

I got bought out. The money won't last very long—you know.

Morally compromised. His shrink had called it—referring to those who purchase in the sex trade; those words came to him now, as he walked away from Coyote. Just then his phone rang! —It was, most unusually, his shrink, calling about some matter of scheduling. He thought about her words; mulled them over.

PM
We are all born down here w/an equal chance, and I do mean equal—for we are given a handicap credit equal to the disadvantage we are also inflicted with. This is why an artist, half mad, has her/his art to retreat into.

Well here is the recount of that Bangladesh horror. The greedy garment manufacturer had built 2 additional stories on top of his factory—to house hundreds of more impoverished wage-slave workers so as to crank out more & more & more money. The additional weight of these brick, concrete & wood floors was not backed up by necessary strengthening of the foundation underneath—because the greedy owner was stupid as well as lustfully greedy. Cracks had been appearing in the concrete walls, which the workers had commented on. The day of the collapse there had been a fierce trembling and shaking of the building, and dozens of them tried to leave the factory floor, & get out of the escape doors to flee but were prevented by the guards who forced them back inside, telling them **GO BACK TO WORK!** Assuming they were trying to leave & not do their jobs. Shortly after the whole building collapsed. Dozens made their way to freedom but the vast majority perished. The workers are still digging them out from under the debris. The greedy owner was caught while trying to cross the border into India. He was dragged back handcuffed between 2 policemen, shaking in fear. It is certain he will be executed. Finally, one young woman has been pulled out alive from under the rubble after 2 weeks. She survived in a small pocket of space, drinking rainwater, and eating lunches of her co-workers who had been killed in the collapse of mortar & concrete. She is remarkably well, and the world is waiting to hear her story!

Troll in the basement is smoking again, its been miserable about 3 hours straight since midnight. It is useless to call in the resident manager on this situation. He never can smell anything. When that problem w/water gushing out of broke pipe under the sink he informed the repair people that: *I could wait until the weekend was over,* and I knew he was either lying or misjudging, and had to snatch the phone out of his hand and scream and scream the actual truth: *the water is gushing out! It fills the bucket every hour! You got to send somebody out right now! I can't sit here bailing this bucket out every hour for 2 days!* --until they sent over a repair person (probably night time double pay.) I had seen the amount of water in the bucket under the sink and had had to change it every hour—the manger's judgment was far off. He is useless thus, in half of all problems. He sides on the cheaper less problematic solution for the management company— which, one day could bring a lawsuit.

So I have to undergo this shit, breathing this shit into my lungs. The man in the basement claims he is not smoking—he is lying also.

Do I have to take all these fools to court again?

If they had never opened up that substandard unit and rented it, this would not be a problem there was no problem of this smoking the first 5 or 6 years I lived here. There are other smokers in the building, but they do not live beneath me!

Currently have fan in the window blowing cold air into my place to clear it out, and me w/a cold!

Oh as a crowning blow—the TV has switched off and can't get it to come back on.

Have prayed for money to God. To upgrade my miserable situation.

Big money!

Sunday, May 12, 2PM
Mouth hurts—from sore on tongue. Filling fell out the other day. (While eating the hard French bread ends.) Pain. Fighting chills & cold.

Spiritual class—we are in the church @ Ephesus—the only church that is doing OK & ready for teaching. Corinthians, Galatians, (You foolish Galatians who has bewitched you?) are in an uproar, as we see by Paul's letters to them!

Morally speaking there's no difference between practicing Christian, Jew, & Muslim, from ordinary people. We all fall short.

Grace appears in Ephesians. Grace is not something you can earn—its given freely, by God.

Spiritual director is like a personal trainer of a fitness, which cannot be observed by the naked eye in any bodily muscles.

> Huge God
> Huge Jesus
> --Participant in class

His tongue was in pain. Communion hymn plays. *Oh God how long I've come here for glimpses of You.*

In the gothic cathedral his eyes slowly looked up, up, up along the grey colonnades into the highest reaches; maybe the Eternal's careful fingers tend over papers w/official seals up there; Red's name and gender change…

PM
Home--& my TV is broke. My house seems empty & dead without a television! Is it truly broke—kaput—or is it simply the need to readjust the converter box—again!

Its exactly 12 midnight, and the heaviness in my air begins again—smoking coming from the basement.

Such misery.

Lay down in bed w/Penny cat—fiddled w/controls—TV working again! Simple press of a single button!

Yeah! TV Back!!!

Monday, May 13, 11AM
Dentist Day. Mouth hurts. Am falling asleep sitting in chair because of pain meds.

Falling asleep sitting down.

1,129, final death toll, Bangladesh. And the workers have stopped digging.

Because of guards who chain-locked exit doors. Execute the owner & lock up all the guards for 10 years. —My opinion.

PM
Nada.

Tuesday, May 14
To his great horror, TM saw by his email account @ Grant Writing Center, that the Bancroft was Direct-Depositing his funds, as he'd asked them NOT TO DO, since 2 direct deposits would kick him off of his Medical benefits *again!* —The stupid Medical jerks can't understand that the two payments are for 2 separate months—despite the fact they both hit on the same month! They cannot average it out! Fucken' idiots! This does not build loyalty to our nation, and for the first time am getting a glimpse why the rich laundry their money thru foreign accounts—so they don't have to pay tax here, because of ineptitude, stupidity, greedy lard-ass officials squatting in their

bureaucratic jobs making life miserable for others on a petty—very petty basis! The rich and knowledgeable just bypass this shit altogether!

A car w/partying jocks burns rubber, skids around corner; big beefy assholes of the privileged class; one holds a 1/5 of Champaign out the window.

Dangerous. Obnoxious.

> You come to SF to party, it's a party city right?
> --Boy toy on Polk Strassa

Lanky young white man carry's tools, expensive; of carpentry, easily on his 6'7" frame dangling from broad shoulders shuffling step on big new boots. —On fast track to high priced job—where is bro black man? Where is the sister?

Hung out in front of Coyote. Have only purchased 1 coffee in the last 2 weeks—so 'po. Talked to folks. No pain—medications effects linger.

One of the old 5 coffee shops appears to be on the verge of opening— all modernized. Wonder if their old grey habitués will return there?

Another—is being painted. Was closed by the health department for vermin on site (again) and supposedly is under new management. Will see what they do w/the place.

The one, w/nice owner on the corner of Pine still not open and no work seems to being done. Some rude young airheads have tagged the place—this compassionate man can ill afford the fines, work needed. These punks are stupid; —not a bit revolutionary, nor do they care.

Coyote—the best of them all, endures.

PM
Today was high; tooth better, but ear aches.

Wednesday, May 15, 11AM

Working last pages COLLECTED POETRY --#1

Shrink day.

Upon success, to not be vindictive—to set things right!

Some individuals give the impression they are caring, kind, compassionate & they are not. Somehow they've mastered the look, the tone & it is truly a deception.

You can tell from the difference.

Priests—they eat @ the finest restaurants.

Don't forget your first love, to do justice!

To do great works—of truth.

Cars honking on Van Ness. Blare of traffic.

OM walks steadily towards Coyote.

His head having been shrunk sufficiently for the week.

He was working towards currency of a higher kind.

The OM had decided against playing the Powerball lottery—which cost $2, on advice of the Eternal—that it could bring trouble of several types.

Mellow jazz plays. Sad refrain. People perpetually sad, existing.

> What would you do?

> I would do great.

He brings 'em down here to show them off. Says one of the OGM. About how the dapper younger Cosmo brings all his boy dates down to sit @ table over a feast of food & drink.

Cosmo circles the block, and its all a bit tired.

The tan skin of his hand lifted Cheetos to his mouth. His fingers, mouth & teeth turned orange from the forbidden Cheetos.

Melancholy flute jazz metronome beats rhythm.

PM
Christ, ugh, arrugh! Am in shitly hell! —Time for pain meds!

Thursday, May 16, 10AM

>Just-before-evening
>   will erase every hostility.
>In the shadows, as a passerby stoops down
>   to pick up a penny---
>   she sees, that she is a giant
>   out of the corner of her eye!
>I'm getting closer to the city
>   where there's fire.
>---THE CITY WHERE THERE'S FIRE—Circa 1969

A person needs raw joy —like the blood of life! They can get it thru their work, their pets, their children. —If everything is going wrong—the kids turn against you, the pets get sick, your work impoverishes you--you can keep from being sad & falling into depression— lift self up thru their spiritual faith.

A lot has already happened today. No NOTES—under the influence—heard that young Junior has been assaulted on the street; his mouth is all fucked up. On one side a big gash deep, to his teeth, and its going to get infected. Cosmo told Junior he should go to the hospital but he wouldn't, said it would heal on its own:

>It'll heal alright—it'll heal from the inside out—that's how the body fights the infection, and it will leave a huge piece of flesh hanging off the side of his mouth.

>A hematobia?

No, worse. Its from the infection. If he goes to the hospital they'll drain the wound, and give him antibiotics then stitch him back up. It'll just leave a tiny scar. But he won't go. He's going to be disfigured.

I don't think he'll live to see 26.

I agree w/that. With the drinking the speed, the drugs, the fighting, and he's homeless. He's not going to make it.

The barriesa carries out a drink for evil young crip* in his wheel chair, sets it out on table, goes back inside. By time the crip lugubriously wheels himself down to table, a passing bum has walked by and snatched it!
*--As opposed to nice & decent crip.

Pleasant conversation today w/Cosmo and 2 older gay guys. But sadly found out some horrible news—Joe is now pushing a shopping cart. He has gone downhill. A shopping cart, —its that bad.

Young & sassy black girls jitterbug past—hope they turn out honest—and safe.

God You're Name is Danger, too! Yes You are the source of danger --& of stability.

Well certainly see how use of narcotics shifts your interests off center. Your intent seeks more pleasure and do less work. Maybe you could hold fast to your most centermost, meaningful work—but less to other things, and even in your most centered works are less innovated, less adventuresome. You let other things go.

I hate to say it, there is no love lost between us FTMs and MTF's. Remember that year we did my play INHABITANTS OF A GHETTOIZED POPULATION, and our great staged rehearsal, given @ The GLBT Center, was not publicized. We were associated w/a trans group of which I was a member, and every affair they were associated w/was well-advertised on their website, and emails went out—but they failed, utterly, to mention our play whatsoever. They did no mailing for us @ all. This was the charge of one of the would-be-

47

women. To this day I do not know her problem. Catty? Getting back for something I know not what? An oversight concerning a person she gives no credit to—because they aren't male-born! Well since the mass-mailing did not go out, in attendance were just 3 people. In a theatre that seats 120. That's right. I don't know if the others up on stage or my ex-wife Jasmin back in the projector room, who was filming were sadly disappointed—but me, I'm use to disappointments as an artist, and as a human being, so I felt little.

One problem artists, writers, actors, beware! Leaving publicity to someone else! Just assuming that after all your hard work, dedication and starvation in the creative arena, that somebody, just somebody has to be able to *get out the word*---- beware! Tain't necessarily so!

So tired.

So, Apple computers crank out 150 million dollars profit *per day* for their numerous applications. OM's writing cranks out some $10 to $50 per month. What is of consequence?

Sometimes street life is less dangerous then tame social forums of the middle & upper classes, the college-degreed ones who let hell go on in civilized manners… between clenched teeth politely back stabbing the life spirit out of some unfortunately naive un-savvy creature.

Well I didn't throw my life away. I did not throw it away!

Well this is my first childhood prayer—to be able to heal someone— my mother in this case. —This is before the forming idea to be a writer, an artist. And subsequently a small publisher! (Of RED JORDAN PRESS!) For as a child I asked for & received a small metal printing press, w/movable rubber type.

PM
Well I am going to tell you something right now, I'm not entirely satisfied w/my digital republishing project, which I've done about 76 ebooks to date—and have around 30 more files to accomplish—and it is a momentous task—I've gotten my stuff Out There, but the OCR process leaves much to desire. This poetry book in particular, it is so hard to format the lines the way they are suppose to be—so its just the

best I can do. If any publishers want to redo it, they must get a copy of AGE OF OM, THE IRON WOMAN; these two volumes in which the original 800 poems were collected, by me in 1996.

Frankly I'll tell you if the reader discovers some misspellings—unless they are cute—they are probably out of my ignorance. Have not had Internet access these last sick days to check spellings of some proper names—like Rama, Bernadette Doran, etc., and am using what I have. This tired spellcheck on my computer is a lifesend, but it has its shortcomings…

I'm gonna tell you, some will say well if you can't do it right, don't do it at all— this is bunk. For a person in my situation it is better to do it not completely right, but at least do it! —Or it will never be done! I must toot my own horn!

You have poetry that didn't hardly sell in the 1970's, and then sat in your boxes for decades and decades, so you come back 25 years later, consolidate it into 2 large volumes, and they go unsold but for the Bancroft Library, and sit and sit for another 15 years—and along comes ebook, so you try, by God, you try again!

Red Jordan Arobateau
Friday, May 31, 2013
2:30 AM, Pacific Standard Time
San Francisco, CA

Part- 2

Friday, May 17

He's cute! You been w/him?

He's straight!

What's that got to do with it? I asked you had you <u>been</u> w/him!

Must say am happy about putting out my first re-published poetry
ebook! Also sold 1 hardcopy STREET DREAMS, and 1 ebook of the
same (w/it's so-poor text).

Blax people are so mean, they hate people.

The hate us, and they even hate themselves. That's why they kill
each other. They're always killing each other.
--Man & his boy toy in conversation

Oh; have acquired a Korean associate, he is a nice young man, very
cute, who all the Old Gay Guys believe is gay, but the young lad has
told me his inner desire—a hot Latina—with whom he will do
Samba—and he will marry & have 3 kids.

If you bring home a wife who is not Korean?

Banned!

And tells me how many children he wants:

2. Yes. One child is one child. Two children is a couple of children.
But 3 is a group. I want a group of children! My family!

PM
Nada.

Freddy said:

Back in the South, we had to call each other *she* around straights;
they were listening to our conversation if we said *he* went off
w/him—so we said *she* went off w/him—that's how we hid what we

51

were really talking about—gay stuff. That's why we called each other she.

The Old Man was wondering: *is my phone broke?* It had not rung in 3 days—tho he'd sent out a series of friendship calls.

It's a party out here @ Coyote—Disco music plays, the queens are all out—after all it is Saturday nite—a nite all we queer family remembers well as a universal fact—tho each of us coming from our own city, our own era; we were all living that nitelife—that gay life.

Cosmo comes along brings his nice young trade out, to show him off.

Lola is here—she looks @ me forlornly—I cannot give her love—because of human stupidity.

Transman sat in blazing sun—cooled by a steady ocean breeze. Beautiful music plays. He called Jasmin—got the recording.

David Young V stops by; robust young man. Just as we begin talking artist shit—how he is having a show @ Café Royale, this high-minded stuff,— there comes on his phone a RANG RANG!

So your toilet bowls leaking… its more then a leek?

Jesus will come down & get you—anywhere.

The Lord assures me I'm a heavy duty player—very heavy duty. The sun baked him---no more friends stopped by to chat—he'd go soon,

Beautiful music cascades over him

I'm waiting to break out—as they say in the business; now unknown, later, known. Break out!

Well I must say seeing David gave me a charge, a spark to jump back into my painting. People need encouragement.

I was at my peek (this decade) when was regularly going to BABYLON FALLING bookstore, in which was surrounded by artists—had artist associates. Must have painted 45 pix!

Gawd. Down the row, Hawk gets in still another fight w/somebody w/his pitbull walking past, sunning herself peacefully then suddenly big Lola goes berserk on her, and the Hawk yells something rudely—when its her beasts fault not the pitbull.

The Owner rushes out holding the two dog-owners apart from each other @ arm length, and admonishes Hawk: *that dog's bigger then your dog!* Owner holds his hands out indicating the two should keep their peace and let it go. The other one goes on down the block. The owner puts his hands on his hips, queenish, and tells Hawk off in a loud voice.

Let me tell you a slight bit what is going on in a certain arena. I as you know by my early JOURNAL, babysat a pitbull for a better part of one year in a facility shelter on Fillmore Street which was wonderful for the animals but very hard on its volunteers, and employees—in fact over the top crazy, jockeying for power positions, obsessive w/animals, to the point of hideous to the humans—none of which is good. I observed about this charming pitbull his great endearing qualities, loyalty, intelligence—and sensitivity. I have never seen a dog get quite as jealous as this one did, to the point of nearly self-combustion—when a dog in his sight got a favor and he was ignored. They have been bred to have horrible defensive/attack hyper aggressive traits, so this again reverts to man, and not a responsibility to the animal alone.

There are 2 pitbull mixes who come up and sit in Coyote.

PM
Arugh. Well stupidly just found out that the Ho's garbage receptacle I so ridiculed for being purposely recycler-proof—are actually *bomb terrorist proof!* They are Homeland Security trash receptacles! Designed to keep any large size bombs being secreted within them!

Had most debased, depraved, dream. Brown skin janitor, taller, sat next to me; w/were talking; turned my head, felt him quickly suck my right nipple on my flat chest, it was very erotic—turned back to look, but he was looking the other way, not moving. He was deceptive. A period of time passed—but just in an instant—I looked to my left, down the worn hall came the janitor—cleaning. But how he was cleaning—he went down upon the floor, flattened himself down; I saw him slithering along the floor; he had grown a long dinosaur like whip-tail which slashed back and forth across the floor—all kinds of dirt, lint, debris was drawn directly to him, magnetically, and his tail, he was sweeping the hall—his mouth opened up on one side and he was stuffing papers, discarded things into it—*cleaning up the corridor* it was truly a horror dream.

Sunday, May 19
Mary Mother of God & Mary Magdalene are 2 different people.

Napoleonic Wars; it was during this time vast amounts of treasure flowed into Europe because of all these conquests.

The Louver is the biggest treasure chest –of looting!

New information about biblical texts is being uncovered in the Middle East. These scrolls—mostly on papyrus—was buried in pots in the sand, hidden from persecution by the established Orders of those times who sent their soldiers out to destroy the Word.

> We have evidence of Mary Magdalene in actual paper products. These paper (papyrus) products are frail. Whole gaps in the Mary Magdalene evidence.
> --Jude Harmon

No images of Christ, and the first apostles until the 3rd and 4th century—until iconography—which was very controversial. Icons of Jesus. There are gaps in the story we can read.

The Greeks took from the Mesopotamians, and the Romans took from the Greeks.

Peace has come! Declare the victors. But it is not true peace, its suppression. This is why war so soon reasserts its evil head.

There are 12 references to Mary Magdalene; first in Mark—who was the first of the gospels written 50 to 60 AD. Luke follows 70 to 80 AD.

It is interesting to note the officials knew the scriptures—backwards and forwards, —for instance the scripture: *he will be raised from the dead.* But those closest to Jesus— his followers, disciples, apostles, those he'd cured from great illness, they did not know this scripture! This is why the knowledgeable officials rushed to Pontius Pilot saying that Jesus' followers would say he had been risen from the dead—to fulfill prophecy (Kings ?) the ancient text, so they should roll a stone in front of the tomb, seal it—and set a guard out over it—so the followers could not come, steal the body, then claim it had been resurrected! They are the greatest fools—but they did know scripture!

> Yes we have the Holy Spirit! The Holy Spirit is in a cage and we've clipped its wings!
> --Marc Stanger quoting the evil ones; those who manufacture church

Maranatha—come Lord come! –From the Aramaic, (bastardized Hebrew).

> Go—in pieces!
> --An idiot @ Grace

White spume of the geyser as Annie Ho & Comrade Red Jordan Arobateau crossed the plaza on way to get her car—to go dining!

Source Restaurant.

Well this is the only way to go! Meat and pain free food! A vegetarian restaurant. W/Annie. No creatures cry out being abused, except maybe the help! Ha ha ha ha ha!

Day after day year after year the same torture goes on—without surcease. That is hell. The ghetto. No change, no betterment. No improvement. No mercy. No justice. All God's goodness and good things—none of it—except @ a price!

55

This is why down thru the ages the good Lord(ess) having installed a conscious in the human race—tugs on various heartstrings and causes them to create waves of protest inside the general ignorant society:

> Against slavery
> For women's rights
> Against animal torture

PM
Avoid all things, which lead to the downward, hell path. Those directly those indirectly. All things, situations, peoples must be examined to see if the outcome w/them leads to the downward path. This is why early warning, or foretelling in dreams sent from The Creator aids us—for if we are warned, we should pay attention to the warning! Then we should take great effort to avoid the subject of the warning! If we are stupid—we should pray God for the understanding, the stamina, to be obedient!

Have been jerking off 5 out of 7 days these weeks, and tonite no exception.

Monday, May 20, 11AM
God awoke him for his casework appointment. My phone still has not rung—despite the many friend-calls have made. I have chilling feeling its ringer might be broken! Any material glitch is always seen as a panic disaster—for me having no money. Maybe Dalora has cut off my phone! Which they've threatened to do for the past several years! This is such a worry! Annie Ho is suppose to give me a wake-up call—but she may have forgot, having problems of her own! Even the pesky pharmacy has not given me one of their dunning reminder to PU your prescription calls!

I'm beat. It's the medication. & hot out today.

Jasmin called me back, that's good. Phone does work. And so good to hear the sound of her voice. My dear friend.

Feel mentally unbalanced. Unsure of myself. Tho not bad enough to make me take tranks. Imagine the soul who must walk around like this 24-7. On big huge-milligram psychiatric tranks.

The pleasant sight of nude men @ Castro & Market Streets is gone. So sad. (Even old fat ugly ones). The engaging sight of human flesh.

OM PU newspaper in the Castro-Mission Health Clinic—he began reading about our ally comrade Hugo Chavez! Aurugh! This happened way back in February! When the revolutionary leader was still alive! This is old newspaper in the poverty clinic.

He went along the underground train station @ the platforms edge; hurried along the platform as he heard the train rumbling behind him—felt very insecure, pushed to the edge by the white tile wall of the escalators. Like he might go flying off the edge into the path of the train.

> Fucken' transgenders. Its like a comic strip.
> --Blax man to blax woman, overheard

Back on the street again, in front of Coyote. Joe, Cosmo. Joe might get permanent housing—all he has to do is go to GA tomorrow—so it is all working out!

Sun hot but wind blowing.

Thank you for your faith.

Blax crows fly thru the air-tossed sky: CAW! CAW! CAW! SCREECH-CAW!

Save your weenie.

People really do respond to money. I see it out here.

Angry shouting inside.

> I want to let you know this line is suppose to be baskets only.

The mean clerk raised his voice in a better-then-you attitude, which reflected race-casting and type-casting and class-casting which infuriated Transman.

> The sign says disabled!

I'm just letting you know handbaskets in…

& I'm telling you it says disabled in this line—why don't you go look @ it!

Well…

Go look at it!

I'm sure you're right.

Go look @ it!

Transman idly entertained the thought of storming back into the Ho's; he went to the new drugstore to PU his script & thereupon told his problems to the very kind Asian lady pharmacist: *I hate this snobby store! The old Calla Market which was here before was so much more natural, more lower down. Greater variety of poorer people.*

So he talked to very nice Patty, supervisor of the Pharmacy next door.

You can always come in here and complain to me! She replied brightly.

Asian lady back in the Ho's was very nice, as he filed his complaint against the dumb clerk.

PM
> When compassion of people of the world is withdrawn it leaves jagged edges---like rocks that shipwreck souls.
> --People who have lost their places? STORIES FROM THE DANCE OF LIFE

Petted cat. She squeaked. Rich grey fur.

Tuesday, May 21, 12-Noon
Life is like this:

> Go to the top of a 1-mile high building. There is a limitless amount of ping-pong balls—of all colors/brands. Just below the top of the

58

building is a series of tubes each of which is quite deep; the ping-pong balls are forced over edge of this building and they each fall into a tube, until all the balls disappear into one tube or another. Each tube has a different consistency. Some are evil dank, cruel. Others joyful fun-filled, happy. The ping-pong balls journey thru their tubes for a number of years/distance, and eventually all will emerge at the end of that tube—just to once again be faced with an amount of new tubes, awaiting their arrival. As the ping-pong balls bounce around each eventually falls into another tube. Again there is a variety of experiences in their journey thru each tube. Some ping-pong balls who experienced such great pain, now find themselves in joy and a wondrous new experience of life. Others who knew nothing bad, now are forced to see the darker side, a different reality. Some experience repeated cycles of the same thing, only eventually to find other realities. These types of cycles repeat and repeat—all the while the ping-pong balls are descending to their life's completion.

At the end all will say they have experienced both bitter & sweet. They have arrived @ wisdom when they know this—and have not been so done-in by one set of experiences that they got stuck in that tube forever.

There are many along the road of life who will call out; *Help Me!* I see now it takes the wisdom of God's instruction we must obey—as to which ones we can help, and which ones we cannot.

Have you got a spare dollar to help me out of my situation? A Blax dike cries in the street. She dances up & down to grab attention.

Coyote.

3 transwomen go past: *you can get a lap dance—as long as you're in the house.*

Lady w/dog exclaims: *Something big is going to go down in this neighborhood, just watch!*

Dream I had foretelling?

Blax man walked by, drug dealer, she eyed him cautiously.

3 trangendered ladies, all the same size, have on a similar dress (male-female style); twitter together on the bench in the parklet. Also present, 5 gays seated all in separate places.

Wind tosses pigeons around in the sky.

Life—what a perfect setting—a background for mayhem, an audience waiting, watching… the still day passing… traffic whizzing along.

Gay men doing show tunes.

It has to play out… Sin has gone out into the world; hurt, injustice, fitting into the divide of right and wrong.

The Lord says *watch!*

& I will be out of harms way of course!

So now I'm going to wait & watch next few days…

Talking about these tornadoes that killed 20 people in Oklahoma: *I'm a tornado when I go down on that dick—*

A white tornado!

Lady w/dog returned: *well;* she seems to think, (reassuring tone) —*it won't play out here, not here—but somewhere…* different drug people crossing the street back/forth. Re-crossing, trying to a make connections.

Something really stupid & mean happens. Big white blue-uniform traffic cop strides into Coyote café, a small gay man zips up in a car, and parks illegally in the motorcycle area—he is dropping off something for the café.

You can't park there; the cop comes out of the café & says. Then walks off down the street—a cunning ploy.

The gay guy nervously backs out of place—but backs into a fire hydrant red zone, perplexed, seeing the cop has walked off; he pulls back into the motorcycle area, runs around to his trunk, picks out a bundle of newspapers, runs into the café. He returns carrying another bundle—the leftovers from last week— but as he throws them into his car, the sneaky traffic cop has reappeared and is writing a ticket.

He had waited for the guy to disappear to come back. This is ugly; bad vibes. The delivery guy should have just driven off, come back half-hour later. He was actually parked only 30 seconds—underlying power play on the part of the cop; no wonder they are hated.

So often I hear these days how the City is getting so greedy, pushing & pushing for money, money, money, making it so unpleasant to do business here—charging $6 for just a few hours parking—while you are inside a café, *spending money* which provides City *Sales Tax* in itself—that business is moving out—expression on the traffic cop's face was stupid, he no doubt is not a well-trained, true SF policeman but a traffic stooge.

Cosmo come by w/his new toy—up from So. Cal.

Red saw a cute but very shabby boy obviously not a toy, not @ this point very cute. Grungy & in desperate need. Sulking along the building fronts, and collapsing dejectedly on the sidewalk next to a wall, dining on a burrito he has scored. Want to get to know him— but not in the naked, biblical sense. I'm curious, interested, compassionate.

PM
Bi-o-biographical. As you see am getting much more into the world of men, and cruising for men, as was in my 20's (always in addition to women). Was thinking in my long history as a fiction writer, did not write many gay men novels:

    BOY CENTER
    WHERE THE WORD IS NO
    ALEXANDER D'ORO
    FLASH ON THE HUSTLER
    THE BIG CHANGE (trans)

Plus about 4 blax straight men novels:

MAN FROM THE BLAX GALAXY
PRISONER OF HEARTS
TO THE MAN W/HAT IN HIS HAND
A BLAX MAN IS NOT A WINDUP DOLL

Now today, my last 3 Journals have been about the man/young-man trade, and cruising hot dick on the hoof in the streets:

LIFE CALLS!
I AM A SOUL
LIFE AT THE BOTTOM OF THE WORLD
THE GROWING WISDOM
STEPS

Wednesday, May 22
A dull ache still remained in the tooth hole.

Old Man saw a slender tattooed oldster w/bleached hair colored lime-green in Mohawk style; his ancient hide is reptile-wrinkled like a coat of skin layered over him.

On another bus, tall man looked like a crack head; long lean body; carried huge backpack full of empty bottles to recycling center—his expression of a crack head, cunning; he twitched, quaked, fidgeted; carried a cigarette lighter which he fumbled with over & over as if could hardy wait to fire up his crack pipe.

Pain; woozy from left-over drug affects.

Smell of construction materials. The luxury condo complex is developing.

Shrink. Talked about dating men, and seeing young men.

Saw the spot I once lived in, age 24. –1968.

I think if you come from family abuse as a child; a child's got a developing brain & during this reign of terror you learn to partially separate from your body---then as an adult it becomes easier to objectify others—separate them from humanness, you don't know what it is to be human!

CAW! CAW! CAW!

Blax crows race across sky @ top speed; far outracing a pigeon.

See Hawk and one of her cohorts. Add news, forgot to say awhile ago. The Malaysian comes up talking to the mean Crip. Very disloyal of the Malaysian—I don't need to be w/this kind of person. Just a few months ago I'd vowed to cut this 'friendship' a loose.

Well just because someone is in a wheelchair don't make them immune from being a bad person, does not automatically pardon them from their social responsibility.

See the kid, head down, hoody hiding him, 2 big trousers w/raggedy cuffs.

Ragged youth shuffle by w/gigantic bedrolls & backpacks.

Seated in hot sun—got up & moved out of earshot of the ugly couple.

Sunbaked.

Another older homeless—he who was once same as the youth— after 30 years has passed w/out intervention nor change of the miserable downward trajectory of his life—shuffles past pulling cart, he stinks of urine.

PM
Nada.

Thursday, May 23
So many millions of dollars have been in the news these days all of them funneled up to a single person or to a group—if all poor people were given a portion of this what a wonderful start they'd have in life.

Talked in sun to some Old Gay Guys.

The finding of self is never a foolish choice. Tho a lot might be lost thru it—severing of our relationship—me & Jasmin when I was frantically searching to find my deeper self.

Not in vain I hope, I pray.

See how the physical youth is, w/no purpose, no motivation for a job –and then again, in old age—pushing a shopping cart.

Just heard horrible news; Joe is pushing a shopping cart.

For months now he has been carrying. Carrying 6 backpacks @ a time; pushing a bicycle bag on wheels full of stuff—from here to there.

> He has all this stuff I have to go pick it up. I don't know why he has all this stuff he keeps collecting all this stuff, he leaves it here, leaves it there —for people to watch—then they loose it & he keeps on loosing his stuff.
> --Cosmo

An elegant pigeon perches on a Ho's railing on one red foot, the other rests, curled into a ball & drawn up into its soft grey feathery underbelly.

He'd spent last 3 hours in sun w/OGM @ Coyote: saw 1 boy toy.

Saw a 2-legged beast come walking along—peeks head under railing—then emerges from under park bench—it is a red-foot grey feathered/downed pigeon w/beady orange eyes.

Told Dr Sam about the fate of a lot of young boy toys. *You can't stay young forever.*

> That path is not going to lead you to a lot of great places—its not good.
> --Dr Sam

Daughter… I come to you over oceans of time…

PM

Nada.

Friday, May 24
They see w/their souls. Not just see thru their eyes.

Tall Asian in Wal-Grims—so nice & super efficient—now how're
you going to compete w/that perfect employee!

Street, frantic honking, car sped past, laid out a layer of grey exhaust
fumes—racing to get to a red stoplight!

Sat w/OGM, am the last one left.

I still have pain in my heart. Unsatisfied by talk.

Pain of daily living, assuaged by talk, camaraderie; is it able, can it be
able to be equal to the depth of the pain of the soul?

Huge blax crow wings upward across sky on mammoth wings aloft
w/morsel clasped in its beak—going to roof roost to nosh.

Mellow jazz plays.

> Some guy was masturbating w/a sword--the gays were making out;
> gay boys; girls were making out... it was just bizarre.
> --Overheard

Patrons discussing HIV; protease inhibitors. Science is marching
towards a cure.

Thinking thoughts over & over about getting to know & help youth
(18 and over) those lost & adrift –w/no direction.

After rehearsing these thoughts over & over he finally managed to
call on God(ess).

A capricious wind nearly took off his cap, while walking home.

Young man Baz came by, took the Old Guy to din @ Crepe place,
then home for expert haircut, beard barbering. Good to see him &
chew the trans-fat.

PM
Nada.

Saturday, May 25
Just saw T-girl I know. She is very successful—for us. Looks
perfect—passable. She works in public world—not in satellite rings
of trans or queer world. She is a success. Said hello by name. Out in
the beautiful sun.

Coming around the corner to Coyote never know what you might
find.

Party of 6 screaming First World white yups in a huge yowling
blockade run screaming across the traffic-run street from their taverns
over on that side to descend upon the humble Coyote, to sit drinking
beer out in the parklet.

One of the OGM says how a noise abatement ordinance has just
passed; the sound level of these taverns must be lowered or their
liquor licenses will be pulled.

Hear the woman's voice screaming—jubilant— over the wind.
Young affluent whites come marching past Coyote on a treck between
their taverns.

Last of the OGM left.

Another semi-blue Saturday.

A lot of tekkis descend onto this global capitol to work in the
startups.* When the startups fail, they leave & go back home.

*--A startup corporation—is experimenting w/new computer applications—
95% fail, but the lucky ones can be sold for multi-millions of dollars.

He saw a pigeon running fast, its feet bound by a wad of human hair,
long strings, lengthy between its legs.

I would free you if I could; says the Lord of power & might

What's a Chinese fire? The howling tekki troop is cracking anti-Chinese jokes. So many, so loud: *how many Chickens have you actually stepped on? What year is it? The Duck! What is the year of the Cat?*

After lovely encounter w/his poetry (THE COLLECTED, Vol. 2) last nite Transman's mind was entertaining thoughts of wining Pulitzer prize... of finally being discovered.

Well, yuh know now SF is becoming known as the party city—

Could be worse.

Yes we could be known as a bankrupt city.

Yeah, like Stockton.

Sleek car pulls up—honks, blares @ the table of tekkies; who scream their response YEAH!

A shrill female voice @ the top of the pack, bellowing—she holds her own.

Inside Coyote toilet, the OM stood @ the urinal, somberly pissing thru his blue disc.

Back outside, the table momentarily empties, then the yups file out of café, each holds 2 handed glasses of beer—*Yahoo...* this is their 3rd round. They've gone from a single drink to two.

Go where you're needed.

PANTS OFF

PANTS OFF

PANTS OFF!

A party city... TWHAK! Beer glasses drop to the floorboards of the parklet. –Smashing.

Donna Summers I Will Survive plays around again for the 3rd track.

Frayed blue jean cuffs, gymshoes, hoodies; large backpacks; a group of less-affluent stroll past.

All of these have that tired grumbling look; overburden by backpacks. *Yahoo,* ha.

The OM gazed back to the table of affluent drinkers—none of them wore gymshoes... The poor who walked by, all had on gymshoes. The poor persons wear. A mark of poverty.

Shake, shake your bootie...

Not a man, but a fairy, in pink, flitted by; an emaciated freak light on his gymshoed feet hovered in Coyotes doorway; flipped her hand, then dashed away down the street, as if in fear.

CRACK CRACK empty beer glasses hit floorboards of the parklet, yahoo!

Hungry, wary, tired, dissatisfied...

Take your passion & make it happen! This is what I've been doing!

The wind picked up noticeably, it followed the same pattern as it always does... blowing harder as day was ending...

Did those human animals who went on different routines, did they knew what he knew? Saw what he saw?

A different kind of bird—Wren? Came up to OM—blax gleaming feathers, twig-size legs.

Drink. OOHHHH! CRASH CRASH of plastic cups of water to the ground.

WHAT THE FUCK'S WRONG W/YOU?

To think these braying assholes are going to be police commissioners & politicians, and are going to be running the world in a few more years…

A dismal day for the OM.

Now evil Hawk has descended. No one to be with & mostly sorrow @ his lack of success.

The one lone female among the pack of jocks is an incredibly groomed preppy; stylish, manicured, pedicured... Coiffeur, red toenails; flawlessly poured into perfectly fitted jeans, affluent casual wear. Pure white polo shirt over an ample bosom, contrast sun-bronze or tanning-booth complexion. Arm in arm now, w/the biggest jock, a head taller then the others; hers is the one w/bellowing commanding voice—it figures.

Position, privilege, power.

    Yahoo! Give it to the bitch!

    That's racist!

Broke beer glasses on the boards.

One of the party walks back to the café on unsteady legs—can see he is concentrating on trying to walk correctly.

Now the man walks past again, this time he is wearing black sunglasses.

    FUCK YOU! YEEAHHA!

Preppies.

Slam bang, 2 more beer glasses hit the ground.

Suddenly a huge roar, one of the men arms flailing, bare hairy legs go up in the air, he falls over backwards and breaks his chair!

The group is well drunk.

Groups of young yups begin to stride back and forth past Coyote—in the street a huge 2-story tall vehicle—a Duck-Mobile 2-decker bus w/ patrons riding inside squawking quackers in their mouths; quacking to blasting music.

3 homeless shuffle past.

The Jolly Olde Pervert disbarks bus, comes over to sit @ table w/OM.

3 trans women go by carrying a couch—sinuous muscular still-male arms straining; they hurry down the street, to which the Olde Pervert exclaims:

> Are you giving curb service now? Lay it down right here—its cheaper; "I'm coming I'm coming, I'm going I'm going.

Fight across the street. 2 men w/a woman between them trying to hold each of the men back; one jock from the party of drinking men on our side, stopping vehicular traffic rushes over —they separate the men, one fighter throws one last punch which lands; his adversary falls down; the biggest of the drinking jocks wrestles the man off, they stop the fight.

Now the drinking party is over. The drunks are sobering up. They hug each other. The ground is a mess of broke glasses, shattered plastic cups & a twisted, broke chair.

Mellow music plays. Women stroll by; the men are all gone

ZZZ livery service drops of some more affluent young.

Its strange how the woman are there in the beginning, and after all the sound and furry of which they are only witnesses or minor participants, after stuff is broke up, and silence finally descends, here come the women once more, striding along w/their backpacks, on more important tasks to do.

PM

Nada.

Saw Mr. Wayne from the sex show on way to cathedral. We walked a bit, then saw a strap on the ground.

> That's gross!

> It looks like a cock strap!

> It is!

> Well not everybody will know that...

Oh ma gawd, oh ma gawd! Listen to this! From Thomas—the Gnostic scriptures; --the Apocrypha:

> Jesus said, I myself shall lead her in order to make her male so that she may become a living spirit... for every woman who will make herself male will enter the kingdom.
> --Thomas 114.

Well our guest speaker on the Mary Magdalene series had a lot of explaining to do about that! (Reverend Professor Rebecca Lyman.)

Before the lecture I waited outside Wilsey Hall w/the speaker and we talked, during which time I gave her my business card. She lectures on gender studies. I told her I was a GLBT writer of fiction and poetry.

The room is filling up w/Magdalene seekers.

Again, a full house.

Social context in the first 3rd or 4th century.

Nor Kamite was found 50 years ago. It contained the gospels of Mary, Phillip, and Thomas. Before, these had been referred to by title—but we didn't have the text. This cache of scrolls was found near a monastery in the desert sands of the Middle East. It appears to have been someone's private collection.

71

Don't know name/who, was collector of text and not sure where it came from. This found in monastery in Egypt.

The Jesus movement in the Hebrew community today.

Early Christianity begins to go out of Jerusalem to India, Rome.

Early Christians were allied w/Hebrew text. They did not have the New Testament —as it was just then being written!

Paul goes into Greece, Turkey.

After 150 AD the movement explodes; this is in which gospels of Mary, Thomas, are written.

Huge creative movement first century after Christ's death.

These documents were circulating—A Bishop of the 4th century said: *these are the only texts you should be reading in private.*

1st century education was very expensive not a lot of well-educated people.

At this period, very few people could read, and very few were affluent enough to have scrolls—and these few were reading all the scrolls circulating at that time.

The third Roman emperor Constantine converted to Christianity in the 4th century, what epiphany did Constantine undergo to cause this change?:

> His mother was a Christian?
> His tutor was Christian?
> He needed one religion to rise up to unite
> all the disparate factions in his empire?

Coptic & Greek mixed, everyday language in Egypt.

Discipline the body.

How did we get here—so that every thing went wrong—The Fall.
We've all been in paradise—but we are now here, on earth, fallen.
Somehow this happened. Wisdom falls into the material world. We
are tempted with the lower material world.

Decay, sin, physicality.

Nor Kamite.

Jesus was not a ghost, or made of pure spirit—he was human. Mary
was brought in to testify that Jesus was born to her—he was a human
child.

Gregory the Great; in the tenth century Mary Magdalene becomes a
prostitute.

Men, the male sex is seen as rational mind—so women need to be like
men.

Rich Hebrew women were the ones who first converted to
Christianity—men were the last to convert.

Widows were powerful. They had money, were not in the control of
anyone. They were no longer under the command of any man, nor
their children.

Later Rome life was a very controlled society, highly visual.

Early century, many Christians were reading all kinds of texts @ the
time.

Early Christian writings.

You are here—that is enough. They sang. What are they saying?
That you are here? (Meaning me.) —Or that You are here?
(Meaning God.) Are they saying God is here, or that you, Red Jordan
is here—and that is enough! Even if am so weak & find it hard to
stand, and have no money to give and have on yesterday's shirt, and
dirty trousers—I am here—

AND THAT IS ENOUGH!

So it was enough that he was here!

OM was tired. He went and sat, all ready waiting, in the pew nearest the lectern, where the sermon and the readings would be soon delivered —instead of mingling together in a circle *gathering* between the baptismal font, and communion table, when the priest in his red/white robes opened the service, and they sang; he saw them, 12 pews away. Due to the sound system the unembodied voice of the priest could be heard floating from out of the grey cathedral walls, hovering in the air over the OM's head—not where it should have come from, out of the priest's mouth.

He saw the visiting priest up close—a well-built Caucasian, his powerful first with a ring—of possession—on the marriage finger. He was privileged.

What OM he had he had earned.

PM
Great Horror—what duefull Chinese daughter has undergone this torture:

> I accompanied my auntie to go purchase a canary. We took the
> canary to her house and after a few weeks it began to sing
> beautifully. Then one day, the auntie's daughter comes over and
> puts the bird in its cage out on the balcony—because the weather is
> so nice. Later, auntie awakes from her nap, and goes out to the
> balcony—and decides to feed the bird. —Foolishly. She opens the
> cage to put in the food, and the minute it opens the bird flies out
> and flies away. I am so angry that auntie would be so foolish—that
> she thinks she understands all about birds! This is the 2nd bird she's
> let escape! If she had wanted to feed the bird she should have
> moved the cage back inside and closed the door to the outside, just
> for precaution! I am so angry, and so hurt—because I am sorry for
> that bird! She thinks its free, but canaries don't survive in this
> weather! And the weather got cold last night, and it is suppose to

be very windy and cold for the next several days! I cannot help but think about that bird in pain, afraid, hungry, lost.

Some people in terrible mental angst, and at the end of their rope, will have thoughts, which convolute, & turn to wounding society—as they have been wounded. And in dwelling on these kind of thoughts, even at first, when they are perhaps less cunning, voicing these dream-like plans to others it is mentioned to them, or they think of it themselves: *what if in you wreaking vengeance on this corrupt evil society you kill harmless beings, thus becoming the very thing you hate and abhor—a murderer of kindness, a murderer of love, a killer of innocence?* At which point the sick-minded sufferer must truly think about this possibility.

At some point in the mentally ill mind, the criminally insane makes a decision to ignore the innocent in their drive towards vengeance on society. At some point in their devolving mind, the idea that in bombing a building, or shooting gunfire into a crowd, that they might be killing some saint, a compassionate soul, an innocent baby—this idea they reject and proceed onward relentlessly with their deadly plot—and whither that mayhem bears fruit the next hour or 2 decades later, still, they have made a decision!

Oh, one of the OGM did a favor for one of the street youths—did his laundry. It was so black w/dirt he had to run it thru the wash again.

Blax moms are up on TV weeping/wailing about their dead sons: *I told him not to go hang out down @ the corner, I made him promise he would not meet up w/his homies; he promised me, & now he dead!* Because he knows how to con momma—to promise—but the moment he's out of her sight he run and do what he wants because the drive is powerful. Mom knows she made her child promise when he was small & she could control him physically. She could put the cookie jar out of reach. She could wait for him after school and lead him home by the hand. Now he's grown, too big to control & too smart, as to lie to mom & promise but do the opposite. Mom needs a much stronger force to intervene & break his drive to destruction. To put him in a locked facility, that will control him until he learns society's rules—to save his life!

Back in the 1960's blax parents in desperation began sending their kids down South to rural areas to live w/relatives, to remove them from the evils of a big city, but to their horror discovered drugs had had made their inroads there some time ago. Here is a similar story about a heroin addict woman we knew in the Gay community:

> I had to kick heroin, it was ruining my life. So I decided to go out to the country to live. I got my welfare money transferred out there, I got a bus ticket. I got on the bus and got out in the boondocks. Nobody there I knew, nobody there hardly @ all; but the minute my feet hit the bus station this drugfiend came up to me and offered to sell me some horse. Here I am 200 miles away in the country & they have drugs there too! Now how that dope dealer know to come up to me! I started right back on drugs the moment I landed there.

Monday, May 27, Memorial Day

> In the soup of creation
> You can't see the human
> @ first.
> They come along later,
> In the evolutionary chain.
>
> Frogs then scorpions
> propel themselves
> thru the murky waters
> with great pushes of their legs.
> Whipping tails
> They swim, searching for food.
>
> God thru creation
> is awaking us.

Am not sure what we are going to inherit, when we inherit the earth.

Coming from the streets the old black expression from the 1970's, they call it *running the streets.* Get into her car driving from club to club to see whose there, having a drink or two at each place, having a party time.

Debarking bus @ Polk, he saw young Junior down the street sprawled against the wall of the Youth Center. Prior, the Lord(ess) had instructed him to get off @ the bus stop there, but being a strong intellect of mind he had disobeyed this fore-warning—so this was the price, he had to walk all the way back down there.

There he lay, talking to a group of his young homies.

Transman easily had could have been out in this street. His strong suite was his father upon whose help he could return too, & on the inside of himself, his essential core of self-perseverance; he having quit drugs & alcohol.

Saw young Hound go by; he is older, more savvy.

> Rock Dove or Domestic Pigeon
> Columbia Livia
> White rump; feral; in places self-sustaining typical birds are grey, w/whitish rump, 2 black bars on secondaries, and broad black band on tail. <u>Feet red</u>. Domestic birds exhibit grey, white, tan, blackish varieties. Voice: familiar to city dwellers.
> A soft gurgling Oo-Roo-Coo
> Where found. Old world origin; worldwide in domestication. West: sustains self in wild about many cities (and in some canyons) in W US, S Canada, Hawaii, habitat: cities, farms, cliffs, nest: on building or cliff. Eggs (@) white.
> -- Robert Tory Peterson first publ. 1934.

Out of whole book full of birds he only wanted one—Pigeon!

Am in the Ho's w/not enough $, spending into rent—young Junior, he is here also, laden w/huge backpacks.

PM
Nada.

Working DEATH FAMILIAR text to the end—have begun editing for ebook THE COLLECTED POETRY –Vol. 2.

Tuesday, May 28, 11AM

As you know I was not alone yesterday, a drear cloudy afternoon—
holiday. Sat w/young Junior & his bulging backpacks (2). In one he
had a Christian Scientist book, containing some scripture, and a Bird
Watchers book, which just quoted for you about my pigeon pals.

Doctor today, and plan to meet w/young Junior baring him that
cellphone I found years ago, which is now obsolete as far as the on-
racing technology highway, but might be worth dollars to some
ordinary folk who needs a basic phone, also a few found trinkets, as
the young man enjoys crafting jewelry.

Well I'll tell you it certainly is nice not being alone. Could have been
blue, fidgeting sitting drinking coffee out in the cold, alone—or
seated in the Coyote window seat, gazing solemnly out, w/no one.
Also expect today too will not be as lonely.

I'm telling you it could have been a lonely blue holiday--Monday, but
was not. Filled w/some agitation about this young man—his future,
also not wanting to get so involved—him borrowing my cellphone,
etc, worries about having 'a transient' up in my place:

> Bedbugs
> Noise
> Shoplifitng
> Possible animals upset

Maybe all needless worries.

2 affluent Caucasian tourists both double-wide w/fat so that they take
the place of 3 humans slowly walking hand & hand block the
sidewalk.

Saw Veronica Combs in clinic. She is looking good… she and ex
wife Jasmin just did a gig together last weekend. Veronica has
switched over to singing, and no more dancing and marvels @ how
Jasmin keeps growing in her rigorous dance---

> We were rehearsing, I looked over and there Jasmin has her foot
> way up to here on the wall doing stretches, and I said *wow how can
> she do that!*

Talked w/blax sistah in waiting room, dug up some old time stuff.
My caseworker happened by and went and brought me an Ebony
Magazine, saying: *here get in touch w/your black roots,* and the blax
sista says:

> You know Ebony magazine was sold to a white man.

> What!

> Yes! Johnson, the founder, he died a few years ago. A white man
> bought the magazine. And then I canceled my subscription.

> Well they're from Chicago, and I remember them… they had a son
> my age… and some other kids didn't they? None of them wanted
> to take it over?

> White man owns it. You can see how it's changed.

> Well at least they're keeping it alive.

We discussed the Black Removal of Fillmore/Bayview Hunters Point,
and how a famous black politician sold blax folks out royally.

SF's getting smaller! See people I know everywhere. Saw one of the
street habitués from Polk down on Market Street, he needed to find
the Bart subway station, was glad to be there to show him.

Sit here—big poodle dog pulling her leash, wanting to see me. When
we are in heaven all will be done. And Afternoon Of A Faun plays.

Sat w/Jolly Old Pervert. We conversed; interlaced w/aplenty of
sayings such as:

> Honk if you're horny.

> I'll pay for that one.

> Here comes dinner.

> I'll take that one—I'll take one end, you take the other.

If you won't go home w/me, there's all that extra money I can spend on him.

And etcetera.

We saw the cute young boy/toys—here from So Cal--& speaking w/young Hound. They disappear down the street towards Sutter.

It must be noted that almost all of the street people are always leaving by going back down towards the TL, never up, where is the more affluent areas.

Must say also, this stretch along the frontage of Coyote—about 75 feet, w/tables chairs against the building, and the garden-parklet on the other side, — can be like a stage show, w/cute men parading back & forth.

Young Irish man we met the other day, is well ensconced in his position @ the Hos, w/40 hours. He has recently added a second job—for a total of 60. So many young people are working 2 jobs! It is necessary simply to pay rent in this Glorious Prostitute of Rent Domination.

Said a friendly word to someone as bright sun beat down in the Ho's parking lot & it made me happy for a moment afterwards. It gets hard being around toxic people—like the two @ Coyote. It is hard on the spirit, and so sad when the big dog tugs on her leash gazing @ me w/mournful eyes—wanting to greet me.

PM
Nada.

Wednesday, May 29
Friend of mine from 40 years past, Joan, was to meet but she calls & cancels—no din din.

A dueful father gives his young children $ out of wallet. Dad.

80

I like to be outside; the kid told me. So many say this—they don't want to be inside their miserable Single Room Occupancy hotels. They idealize the outside as raw freedom!

Bus went by the Youth Drop In Center, on way to Shrink. Saw Cosmo w/2 young men leaving out of the Center carrying boxes of their stuff to put in his trunk.

Around some Youth Centers there has been installed a quarantine area, of city blocks, or hundreds of feet, inside which no adults are allowed. —Because pimps, pushers, dealers of every stripe, tricks— would wait outside for the tender young youth—and all their troubles to emerge— to devour them.

This is a sign posted on the Youth Facility around corner from Café:

Overage youth please respect the 2-block radius rule!

What is the end to adult—kid relationships of dubious kind? See the youth age 14; then age 20, then 35, then 45—do they make it to 50? What have they done w/their lives? What is the impact of receiving moneys, gifts one has not truly earned but by their good looks and youthful unspoiled bodies.

Am questioning about this issue; you see it in movie stars, too—who are deified. What is the end result? Spoiled or profiting?

Saw priest Will, he had startling news, —he is leaving St. Cyprians.

So this was the result of the angst we'd shared together!

But he was not sure where he was going.

Be honored if a bum asks for spare change—instead of angry.

For you work.

Young man on the bus asked if I had 25¢. I said: *I need 25¢*; irately: *in fact I need a dollar…*

81

Gigantic blax crow sits on toppermost of the egregious 75-unit condos squawking!

Shrink.

Well Shrink & I discussed sexworking briefly—she tells me the longevity of a female sexworker can last well into her 50's, 60's—whereas the men has had it by 30.

So strange—walk along the streets, avenues, writing NOTES see so few others do this---& those are all mentally ill.

The OM contemplated, as he steadily walked uphill from Shrink to hangout in Coyote that humans walked, feet on ground—feet, that 3 billion years ago was a tail. Their head on top. Where as, fish propel by fanning their tails back, forth, and their head is out in front.

Talked to young Junior; said he had sold guns. Long conversations on projectile range, calibers, hollow point bullets, the damage it does to the body and etc. He has given up selling guns; this is progress.

He doesn't wash his clothes—just wears them until they wear out, then he gets new* ones.
*---Freebox donated, 2nd hand.

> Spread those legs baby—a big canon coming.
> --Red's perverted mind

A friend calls to invite me to blax T-man party across the water & I stated:

> You will not catch me back in Oaktown again—unless SF is destroyed by fire.
>
> By yuppies.
>
> That's right! Until SF is destroyed by yuppies!

PM
60% of the world's population has never flown in an airplane—.

Giant Sequoias 28-stories tall—2,300 years old. They are the world's tallest trees.

Our planet earth is 4.6 billion years old.

Thursday, May 30
Just recalled one of my numerous jobs was working upstairs in the Flood Building, —epicenter downtown Market Street @ the Cable Car turn-around. A plethora of severely mentally ill of all stripe abound there, and I was so moved, began preparing sandwiches for the homeless & brought them in a bag and distributed to those seated on the cold cement.

> The T Thing
>
> Every room I walk into
> it's the T-word, well,
> what do they think I am?
>
> Every person I meet, its always
> --the T-thing.

Just back from blax art gallery—said she (owner) had flown out of town again. Left my card. But the young white man who received it, told me, actually it was he who was the curator, not her, who judged the entries. And I thought:

> A potential gate-keeper. If he looks @ my site and finds out I'm T, he might hate me, and just throw my card away.

T man was unable to eat found-sunflowers, no teeth; which improperly came down one upon another.

Talked to the Malaysian, who stopped by—baring a gift, sox.

Somehow we were talking about the same topic as me & therapist and some others about very young beautiful people having sex for money and favors from older men, and none of them seems to think it's a very good idea.

They just want youth—but that runs out.
--The Malaysian

Saw brother Jay & sister Kathy from church, showed them my prints of my pix.

> Said of my postcard BLUE JESUS w/Jesus holding a tiny church in both his hands-- Don't take the church in @ the service then leave, take the church w/you.
> --Kathy Stevens

Saw young Junior –late—said: *I'm going home to sleep.* Told him: *I'm very glad.*

Old speed freak burnt-out brain preaching gibberish in the street.

Ohhhh AH HA—the soft gentle voice of an MTF transsexual—a mad one—as she leans against the wall of hospital—St. Francis.

PM
OH MUTHA FUCKER! Said the OM, *Oh Muthafucker!* He told the Lord(ess), the OM had been gazing down on an ear wax which now lay on the flesh of his forefinger—how it had, once being so stuck, managed to come falling out of his left ear (the difficult one). He marveled at the wondrous workings & interconnections of the human body and how it all worked, and how the Lord(ess) had set it up—thru evolution probably. And was idly wondering: *how did you do this?*

I figured it out. The Eternal had replied.

So of course OM was highly impressed @ such a great Mind which could figure all this stuff, out so far in advance… what a giant Brain the Eternal must have! A Brain beyond human comprehension!

Friday, May 31
This society is so cheap so the money I get always runs out & is never enough & the rents are growing astronomically; asking too much—so the inhabitants are constantly in a state of anxiety to panic if they can remain in their houses—their stomachs grinding w/hunger in self sacrifice to afford their last penny all to the rent, while those who misuse them are well-fed.

Grungy street kids.

Sat w/OGM, young Junior came by, we talked a moment, I gave him $2, (my last), for food. He is out hunting for money for rent—apparently this free room deal has fallen thru.

PM
Nada.

Saturday, June 1

> Yo' want the tennis shoes without no sox—they gonna stank! They gonna stank!
> --Tenderloin.

> OH LALA HAWWWWWW HAKKAH OWWWWWW!
> --Street

Transman walked to the PO, mailed off his Bancroft offerings, then rushed towards the cafe.

One of the corporate's security black/red cars drives past—a social worker told me the T about this:

> They are set up by a group of large hotels, and small Muslim markets. They are prejudice. They shove homeless people around. They are violent. They threatened a blax man w/a baseball bat. They are unlicensed by the City.

The OM marched in hot sun from downtown Post Office to Coyote—but did not feel dizzy.

Malaysian said: *I find myself PU coins on the streets—find more coins on the streets then I do playing the Super Lotto.*

Saw the Scottish lassie in Crack House Café. She just moved out of her wonderful apartment—*it was time to go*—she says. Bought out for $25,000. The owner wanted it. Under rent control, her rent was $1,200—they will rent it out for $3,500; she has options of other housing tho, which is a true blessing.

So now have heard varying buy-out prices. This is going down in this greedy city. Anyone w/out many resources like me, on the bottom of the barrel certainly should not spend down this lump sum of cash—which they might never get again, but go to legal steps to put it into a managed trust and continue to live on their regular income—which means finding cheaper lodging then where they had been, and this will inevitably be smaller, without cooking facilities maybe, no private bathroom or kitchen—having to share all these facilities down-the-hall.

PM
What an upset! Got to pet shop—found no Crank of America debit card! Aurrgh! Am usually so careful!

The OM, staggered out of the shop w/small bag of cat treats, being all he could afford in cash, and went directly to the Hos, where he inquired @ desk was a debit card found? The polite young employee manager went to another counter, and out of a drawer produced a wad of Left-Bank Cards. It was amazing how thick this wad of lost bank cards was! His was not among them. Transman began to rack his brain—where had he been, what shops had he patronized, what bank branch might he have stopped by, inadvertently leaving card there?

Purchased his cheese, sparkling water—to go w/the cheap pork. — Chicken hot dogs, —and there, midway thru the Ho Sto' he recalled being at the Infernal One, photocopying! Gave them a call—sure enough! They had it!

In my minds eye I see, remember the artists I've known; remember the works I've seen, the poetry I've heard them recite in basement grottos after hours —seen them creating it, sweaty pencil on paper, line by line. I heard them deliver their poetry @ parties, performing in silhouette, black fingers gesticulating against strobe lights, witnessed it. I spent hours with them days, weeks; was lovers w/some. Yet today you don't know who they are. History does not have them. They have fallen thru all the cracks—only a few remember them, and nowhere are they recorded. You have me tho, misspellings & all!

Sunday, June 2,
Class taught by Kate Cooper, professor of antiquity, Manchester,
England.

> Some of the fragments of the gospels of Mary housed in archival
> boxes for decades, were discovered once again, by a young
> researcher looking thru them for a university project.

What this means is a substantive archeological discovery was dug up
in the sands of the Middle East in 1950's. Scrolls, documents,
preserved for 2,000 years in earthenware, were catalogued. Some
were researched, other piles of fragments were categorized & put into
archival boxes, and there remained in the collection—waiting to be
patiently shifted thru, translated to see what they were. And now, @
turn of the 21st century they were translated and printed.

Jesus was born in a Roman province.

Lacking information, each town is separate from the next---this
failure to easily transmit information is illustrated on a map, the
distance from Rome to Jerusalem is just 2 inches… But it was hard to
get news out—there was no writing, but expensive papyrus, which
took a long time to copy.

People in the cloth trade, especially women in the cloth trade were
resources which helped the Word, as it was carried by the disciples, to
move on to the next town. Female boat owners also were supportive.
As said, there was lack of information, or inability to reproduce text—
so it was conveyed by oral tradition for the first 120 years.

By first 500 years nobody has any idea what anyone else was
saying—for little was written. There were no photocopy machines,
no printing presses. No way to transmit knowledge but by word of
mouth. The Oral Tradition.

The Cannon took 400-years to construct. This means what was going
to go into the bible, or not.

A cannon of scripture.

Original emperor Constantine 272-337 AD, instituted Christianity as the Roman State's official religion.

Constantine retuned goods, which had been stolen from the early Christians.

Idea of Jesus' resurrection from the dead did not become a disputed church issue until 200 AD. Up to then there was only concern w/spreading the Word.

Female property owners appear in census 114AD.

Female property owners were often bullied by their male neighbors. Men tried to steal the lands or goods of their women neighbors; this is documented in litigation records of the times.

The church was constantly beset w/argument to whither women should have authority.

Debate about women authority rages on, & on to our modern day war over Female Priests.

Repentant sinner theory's didn't get attached to Mary until 600AD Gregory, w/his doctrine of The Repentant Prostitute.

> A person who is in the weaker position often has a testimony, which is precious.
> --Quotes from Kate Cooper

Scrolls from the 4th century was found, which had been hidden by a group of monks— famously called the Gnostic documents; however there was probably no Gnostic religion.

All these found documents are 2, 3, or 4, out of thousands of different theologies in play.

For centuries warring factions were trying to get the book of Revelation taken out of the bible, but they could not.

De A Kio Nawe: (Greek)

> To provide for
> To take care of
> To offer our own resources
>> & provide for
> To be a pastor.

> Deacon

Elephantine columns; the massive legs of our Mother God covering us, protecting us, feeding us. Un-embodied voice of the priest boomed out of new speaker in front of OM—tho he was sitting way off in the mahogany pews, and the priest was far off, standing back beside the communion table which as you know is set on the eye of the ancient labyrinth.

> I am astonished that you're deserting so soon the gospel you've been given.
> --Scriptures

> Those who come among us setting out a gospel that is not the gospel of Christ.
> --Scriptures

He truly was moved by the service so that he had to fight back tears.

PM
See movie on conservation of Redwoods on the California coast—largest trees on earth, there is a natural deep water basin under that part of California, enabling the giant's roots to feed on water all year round.

There are obnoxious pictures of grinning loggers from the 1800rds and early 1900rds—in rough clothes holding axes, saws, they have been chopping down 1,000 year old giants—making some logging clear-cutting firm incredibly rich, and giving themselves a paycheck wage. —While destroying one of earth's greatest treasures.

Well here I go, must do this!:

THE GOSPEL OF MARY
Following Papyrus Berolensis 8502 Saec V)
Edition: Christopher Tuckett, Oxford University press 2007

7 (sections follow the Berlin codex's page numbers)

Will matter then be destroyed, or not?

The Saviour said; 'All natures, all forms, all creatures exist in and
with each other and they will be dissolved again into their own
roots. For the nature of matter is dissolved into the roots of its
nature alone. He who has ears to hear, let him hear.

Peter said to him, 'Since you have explained everything to us, tell us
this too: What is the sin of the world?'

The Saviour said, 'There is no sin, but it is you who perform sin
when you do what is like the nature of adultery which is called sin.
Because of this, the Good came among you to the things of every
nature, in order to restore it to its root.'

Then he continued and said, 'That is why you are sick and die, for…

8

of the one who… he who understands, let him understand. Matter
gave birth to a passion, which has no image, which proceeded from
something contrary to nature. Then there arises a disturbance in the
whole body. That is why I said to you, be obedient, and if you are
not obedient still be obedient in the presence of the different forms
of nature. He who has ears to hear, let him hear.'

When the blessed one had said these things, he greeted them all,
saying, 'See here! Or 'See there!' for the Son of Man is within you.
Follow him. Those who seek him will find him. Go then and preach
the gospel of the kingdom. Do not

9
(9.1-10.14 also attested in P. Oxy 3525)

lay down any rules beyond what I have appointed for you, and do not give a law like the law-giver lest you be constrained by it.' when he had said this, he departed.

But they were grieved, and they wept greatly saying, 'how shall we go to the Gentiles and preach the Gospel of the kingdom of the son of Man? If they did not spare him, how will they spare us?'

Then Mary arose, greeted them all, and said to her brothers: 'do not weep and do not grieve nor be irresolute, for his grace will be wholly with you and will protect you, But rather let us praise his greatness, for he has prepared us and made us into human beings.' When Mary said these things, she turned their hearts to the Good, and they began to discuss the words of the Saviour.

10

Peter said to Mary, "Sister, we know that the Savior loved you more then the rest of women. Tell us the words of the Saviour which you remember, which you know but we do not, and which we have not heard.'

Mary answered and said: 'What is hidden from you, I will proclaim to you.' And she began to speak to them these words, 'I', she said, 'I saw the Lord in a vision and I said to him 'Lord, I saw you today in a vision.' He answered and said to me: 'Blessed are you, for you did not waver when you saw me. For where the mind is, there is the treasure.' I said to him, 'Lord now does he who sees the vision see it through the soul or through the spirit?

The Saviour answered and said, 'He does not see through the soul nor though the spirit but the mind which is between the two is what sees the vision and it is... (missing pages)

15

... it. And Desire said: I did not see you descending, but now I see you ascending. Why then do you lie, since you belong to me?' The soul answered and said: 'I saw you but you did not see me nor recognize me. I was to you simply a garment and you did not know me.' When it had said this, it departed rejoicing greatly.

Again it came to the third power, which is called Ignorance. It asked the soul, saying: "Where are you going? In wickedness are you bound. Indeed you are bound. Do not judge.'

And the soul said: 'why do you judge me when I have not judged? I was bound though I have not bound. I was not recognized, though I have recognized that the All is being dissolved, both the earthly things.

16

and also the heavenly things.'

When the soul had overcome the third power, It went upwards and saw the fourth power: it had seven forms. The first form is Darkness, the second Desire, the third Ignorance, the fourth is the jealousy of Death, the fifth is the kingdom of the Flesh, The sixth is the foolish understanding of the Flesh, the seventh is the wrathful Wisdom. These are the seven Powers of Wrath.

They ask the soul: 'Where do you come from, killer of men, or where are you going, conqueror of space?'

The soul answered and said: 'What finds me has been killed, and what surrounds me has been overcome, and my desire has been ended and ignorance has died. In a world I have been released

17 (17.4-19.5 also attested in P.Ryl 463)

from a world and in a type from a heavenly type, and from the getter of oblivion which is only for a time. From this time on, I will attain to the rest of the time of the season of the aeon in silence, since the Saviour had spoken with her up to now.

But Andrew answered and said to the brethren: 'Say what you say about what she has said. I myself do not believe that the Savior said this. For these teachings seem to be giving different ideas.'

Peter answered and spoke about these same things. He asked them about the Saviour: 'He did not speak with a woman without our knowing, and not openly, did he? Shall we turn around and all listen to her? Did he prefer her to us?

18

Then Mary wept. She said to Peter: 'my brother Peter, what do you think? Do you think that I thought this up in my heart, or that I am lying about the Saviour?

Levi answered and said to Peter: 'Peter, you have always been hot-tempered. Now I see you are arguing against the woman like the adversaries. But if the Saviour made her worthy, who are you then to reject her? Certainly the Saviour knows her very well. That is why he loved her more then us. Rather let us be ashamed and put on the perfect man and acquire him for ourselves as he commanded us, and let us preach the gospel, not laying down any other rule or other law beyond what the Saviour said.'

When

19

… and they began to go out to proclaim and to preach. The gospel according to Mary.

So it seems all this is a gigantic puzzle—fragments of papyrus unearthed in the Middle East, to be assembled into knowledge of the very foundation of given wisdom by the Eternal thru Her/His Son Christ, Jesus, and told to the Apostles---the first fleshly witnesses of the Ministry, including Mary Magdalene.

> @ the Mercy Seat of God; the convent where nuns sit in penury, perpetually high up over the grounds @ St. Paul's; forgiving telemarketers, liars, hookers, transsexuals, and other heinous criminals…
> --PASSAGE Vol. 5.

Red Jordan Arobateau
Thursday, June 27, 2013
1:30AM, Pacific Standard Time
San Francisco, CA

Part- 3

Hate is so virulent, so real—people run from it—and move out of town to avoid it and relocate to a different state to get away from its effects. They might leave a whole continent to go to a nation, which is free.

Monday, June 3
Transman sat in front row; sees, hears! —Double duty lecture on Marriage.*
*--Given by Reverend Professor Rebecca Lyman & Reverend Dean Jane Shaw.

Idea that marriage is irrevocable vow before God—is not in the bible—Roman & Jewish law, perceive marriage as a contract—a contract which can be dissolved. Most lawyers say you cannot set up a contract unless it can be dissolved.

A vow is eternal, & irrevocable.

A marriage is a contract. A contract in the bible; not a vow.

The idea of marriage and the Christian church didn't come about until the 5th century in Africa—a bishop there answered the letter of a petitioner:

> The man's wife was not expected to live, she took to her death-bed and there took the vow of celibacy—but, she lived. The man wrote to the bishop asking was the vow still valid, and would his wife have to be a celibate forever? The bishop replied; no, because her vow had not been recognized by him, as a priest, nor the church.

Paul thinks the end of the world is coming @ any time—*now*; so he'd rather not make any marriages or contacts but he realized many of the congregations were on fire and had to have companionships/ partnerships to keep them out of sexual trouble, until the world ends.

Paul was a Roman citizen & Jewish rabbi @ the same time—. Thus his information had greater depth then many, and made him a more powerful person.

Jewish law is polygamous & wants a man to be responsible to all his children, as many of them as possible whether by his married wives or other women.

Roman was only responsible to children he had by his wife.

Roman procreative rules which women's children are going to be protected.

Roman law & Jewish law differ—Jew encouraged to marry as many women as possible & be responsible to all his children.

Jewish man was accountable to all his women, and a married Jewish woman is accountable to one man.

Roman & Jewish always said marriage was for the sake of children.

1215; church becomes the church we know today. It was then get we marriage sacraments by the church.

From 1215 began the idea that marriage must be under sacraments from the church.

Before 1215 marriage was just between 2 human beings, a contract—the church could care little about it. —The clergy was advised not to interfere with common peoples business between each other, and this, marriage, and romantic liaisons was considered non-clerical domain.

4th century monasteries begin to develop celibacy—idea begins to come in from 400AD to late in that century.

With the American Constitution, equality in America is instituted by the founding fathers, but there are some problems. What about slaves, what about women?

1930 council of Anglican Church, the Landebeth Council, there was written the first idea that marriage could be for a relationship between woman and man *not having children*—this of course set the stage for same-sex unions.

A lot of the rules were for control, dominance by men.

A priest sees all profoundly sexist positions, counseling men and men couples or male and female couples.

In the bible there is written; no reason, no grounds for, no evidence, nor is it seen as vital, --there is no definition of marriage!

State church began to exert more control over marriage. Prior to that church made a point to say this marriage is between the 2 people; it is *their* marriage, not the churches.

Over 100 different rights afforded to married couples & not to civil unions. This is why its so important for us to have marriage rights!

Bishop of Luxemburg definition would get heterosexual marriage rights; & none of this would be an issue.

Pray and pray always.

PM
Text ebook editing COLLECTED POETRY –2

Oh ma Gawd! Thinking back about the class tonight—spoke that:

> A contract can be changed. There is no legal contract that can be set up without the understanding that at some point it can be revoked.
>
> A vow cannot be revoked.

Oh Jesus H. Christ! So this is why I cannot end my vow of semi-poverty! It would take major praying, davaning on this subject! –Not simply to just change my mind!

I recall the many nights getting down on my knees and beseeching the Eternal—if S/He would only bless the tiny animals, the horrendous afflicted of this earth, that I would do my part by giving up my component in this race for greed, for acquisition, hence my vow of semi—tho not complete— poverty!

I have made a vow—a very hard thing to break! And a Vow To The Eternal! Well! I guess this explains everything!!!!!!!

AURRRRRGGHHHH!!!!!!!! And, the Lord(ess) gently speaks to me, that I should be of great joy… S/He is pleased!

I think I've said it very plainly by now—I think I've made my statement very plainly & very purely; I'm a human, as a human I make all kinds of foolish assumptions which later prove to be wrong. – You can see them right here in my Journal JOURNEY series; e.g.:

> March 30th:
> Black is white!
>
> March 31st:
> Black is purely white!
>
> April 1st:
> Duahh… Well… white is actually black!

Stuff like that—*realizations*— which come later. The hindsight of wisdom.

The Growing Wisdom!

I've laid my hand down on the table that I'm working for God and seeking up the path God travels, following the Holy One, seeking no power other then God the Most High.

Lot of artists push the border of insanity, we are right up against it—but we are not insane; ---afraid of this in ourselves; in some this is so intense that they step away from their artistry, cover it over as a squirrel buries its food for another season.

A season, which never comes.

Because we access part of the brain others can't or won't do people say: *dude where you get the idea for that stuff!*

Its because we're half-way crazy.

Tuesday, June 4

Wind blowing, walking out on my Journey downhill to pay Infernal Rent, & watch for pennies—might be $3.49 cents short when all shit comes in—rent, website, etc.

Bingo! Found 25¢, then a penny.

Hey white girl!

Hey blax man!

TL hotel, 2 big cops—a stabbing? Investigation.

Blax street man ambles over the stinking street; 2 large beer cans hi-octane beer, stuffed 1 in each hip pocket he takes up ½ of a whole sidewalk stretching out his big arms & legs, and more humble people are afraid to pass him by.

Low hung pants like a baby walks w/diaper.

Birds sail majestically in air over clearing of low-lying motels, garages.

On wei to the Infernal Rent Property Management—what better place to stop but by Socialist office where I found that Comrade Karl Marx had already written about landlords—extensively. Hope to download some of his free writings and re-print them into one of my journals, credited, soon! So! I'm not the only one! (Who observes a infinite hatred towards these corrupt enslavers.)

Well if I had not walked these streets as a poor person, would I know?

Relentless—the word for rent going up up up up, every year whose rate is proscribed by law, and not the spirit of community.

2 more cops on Van Ness Ave, 6'3" burly chests packed w/bullet proof vests. Service revolvers in holster on harness strapped around their own ordinary pants belt; dangerous automatic killing machine, it

has killed many crooks & innocent fools as well. Be careful of the cops in blue uniform!

He stopped to feed pigeons bread in front of real-estate mogul/art college pimps affluent display of Rolls Royce's in her showroom on Van Ness Ave.

Cute gay man who flirts w/me, as we shake hands, his warm & thick, he tickles my palm w/a finger: *Means I want to fuck your brains out;* cute slightly older barkeep in the new bar opened down on Post/Polk. Does he know I'm trans? Does he tickle every man's palm?

OM sat in a Coyote picnic chair. He ate the sandwich meant for Junior—who had not showed for several days. A crumb dropped. Pigeons flew down. Where there was one head bobbing was now a dozen—for food.

Fed pigeons crumbs looking over his shoulder for signs of the Owner. It might get him into trouble, but it would not keep him out of heaven!

Two poorly transitioned T girls gracefully walk past:

> Drop In Club offers a stage every Thursday.

> What?

> A stage.

Shows, and glamour, tinsel and fake. Surfaces.

Our meager world.

Oh no! The baby pigeon has taken roost between my feet—small, without a tail bedraggled, its pink flesh shows thru torn feathers.

Its with its flock. Said the Lord. So Transman felt relieved, that the bird would fly upward, to safety.

A work of compassion.

Talked to TG girl he knew—they sat in Ho's where sun went in/out. This woman, his own age, now, 60's is very passable. She was put in a mental institution as a child, for being a 'boy' who acted like a girl. It severely impacts all the rest of her life.

I'll eat the Word of the Lord(ess) up for breakfast, lunch & dinner. I'd rather eat God up in person but the Word will have to do until the real thing comes along.

PM
Just looked @ my foodstamp receipt. $30. It is not enough to feed me until Grace Grant comes in! This is such a nightmare. Am busy in process of hiding my money. They think am earning more then I am!

Ghetto connotes to many a place of poverty. If the word originated among the Jews of Italy 300 years ago, it would be, like my own upbringing, in a bourgeoisie section—a *segregated* black section of South Side Chicago—a place of both rich *and* poor—but all of us in quarantine, forbidden to buy housing outside its confines, nor even to walk there.

Wednesday, June 5, 1AM Shrink Day
Waiting for Junior while Cosmo turns a date w/him.

Was suppose to spend time doing art w/Junior.

Junior/Cosmo call—but he has to go buy dope w/the money he's just earned—somehow this whole thing canceled until tomorrow.

Here is some of what has been said in the last days:

> Cosmo enables them. He gives them money for sex then they go buy drugs w/it. He keeps them high. It's not money for food. He gladly buys them food. But the money he gives them—that's what doing the damage.

PM
Had fun today outside, Polk Strassa. Went there from Shrink—little Junior was there, 3 OGM, plus Cosmo. We had fun.

Oh, the good Doctor called last night, and out we went—to Good Vibes, the Sex Shoppe you will remember of Rosa Salazar in PASSAGE, my beginning JOURNEY Journals. Thereby I got 2 ribbed condoms and he got XXXXX. (Classified Information!) We coffeyed and he gave me or loaned? $20, which will save my life.

Thursday, June 6,
On wei. Sam gave me $20, thank God, proceeded to add to bus card, got cat treats (which is the only thing she will eat eagerly) and Swiss cheese to add to tonites precooked meal of beans, beef soy chorizo.

A stalwart artist, David Young V strode by Coyote and I got the location of one of his recent murals—to take young Junior by.

A big girl on tall shoes tipped into Miss Coyote; she was a big buxom white gal & carried a very tiny purse—all matching outfit, purse, shoes, skirt, & blouse. Big girl; *tiny* purse.

Pigeon came –walking--- yes waking across the busy car-filled street—on its afflicted feet. He saw then, they were tied together loosely, so it could hobble, but not walk proper. The desire for life propelled the pigeon forward— for Food!

I'm hungry. Stated a voice in the alley.

Fly or be crushed.

He prayed for the pigeon that soon it would fly: *Jesus uplift this pigeon in Your hands—so it can fly up to safety in a ledge above.*

So we will pray for the challenged people among us—that they too gain their wings & be lifted up --& not be crushed by the evil in this world.

Junior came rumbling along w/gigantic backpack on rollers, and a blax friend from Texas—talked to the brother, asking was he looking for work, at which point the savvy 35 year old took it to mean sex work—by which I hastily added: *I mean the work where you get Social Security.*

Oh, paycheck work. Yes. I was in XXX corporation, for 15 years.

He will get employment, and will succeed; it's the young Junior I am concerned for.

Saw Joe, he was on his way to do sex work—we exchanged a hug. I told him: *I don't have any money and won't have none until August.*

The battered young pigeon hobbled over—it was then I saw its feet were tied—bound by some string or web of hair, which it'd stepped on in the streets.

The OM fed the baby pigeon repeated morsels of Cat Delicacies—just purchased— and it soon learned to open its young beak & swallow them up whole. The pigeon was very well fed by about 15-morsels before the afternoon was done. He wanted to figure out a way to catch it, & cut the string that bound its feet—the Lord(ess) told him it would break in time.

He prayed to the Most High.

The little pigeon had left drops of blood over the cement pavement— bright red drops—its feather was bleeding.

Junior & his blax crony left pulling gigantic pack on wheels. The OGM had all left. Day was done.

PM
There will be suddenly in your Christian journey a time that the scriptures become alive! You step right into them—in real life. The everyday doings in God suddenly become anointed, part of the mixing together of time zones, dejavu; you are walking & talking—wrapped in scriptures, and nascence miracles begin to transform into reality.

I have just consulted my calendar and see that tomorrow, Friday (Shabbat) we were invited to Sheriff Israel to study the psalms—yet I have a work in progress, young Junior, who has quoted to me the 23rd Psalm about 3 times now. He is handsome, young, buoyant. In his pursuit of drugs—enabled by turning dates w/men 40-plus years older then himself, he will one day become addicted, unattractive or dead.

His market value will have plummeted South like a limp dick.
Worthless—but to those who study the human heart.

> Red: I don't like being a person who fixes up dates with people—it
> makes me jealous, but you do know that XXX (the Jolly Olde
> Pervert) has been looking for you, and that's $35 dollars.

> Junior: Yeah, but I don't want to now, it does strange things to my
> head. I can't go up there right now.

It was ironic, @ one point the tall guy who was practicing fitness in
his older age exclaimed how exhilarated he felt from being on
exercise machines @ the senior center: *I can take on any 5 men! Let
'em come @ me!* But just then, of all people the *Owner* came out
wearing a dour expression—w/a twist of sardonic and announced: *I
don't like people.* Which certainly is strange for someone in the
service industry who makes a living catering to the needs of wining &
dining customers…

Editing GROWING WISDOM –2, which brought the Korean to mind—
and I do believe after observing this young man carefully, that he is
probably more gay then he admits, or wants to show. He might know
he is gay but the family demands are much too strong. He will marry
an unsuspecting younger Korean girl, not experienced, and work on
having his family while continuing an undercover gay sex life. He
will be discovered, as all are, and many tears, separations, disasters,
disgraces will follow.

I think the fact that the upper echelons of the staff was getting such a
big salary—compared to the tiny little stuff they were giving us—
another aggravation why am not at that tranny spot no more.

I feel a bit lonely tonite—and ineffectual. Heart feels faint—literally.
Would be so nice to have one of these handsome young sex workers
w/me—but have no money. Plus the growing awareness—any money
I give is not towards rent, nor food—but to buy drugs—the thing
which is drawing them inexorably downward—into an inescapable
pit.

It is fun now, but won't be for long.

Anyway, this is how I feel.

Friday, June 7
Animal control told me that people catch unsuspecting pigeons and tie their feet together. So it is not a young bird who strayed into string carelessly placed by a human, but cruel intent.

Oh, also found out, Pigeons are property of our US Government! They are protected!

Tranny girl beautiful bronze skin waddles by on flip flop sandals bare legs; like an ugly ducking walking towards Swandom—electrolysis in process.

PM
Nada.

God is Center of centrifugal force—your work should be centered around this Core—God, —all else is off to the fringe, is flying outward; off, away into oblivion, shattering thru outerspace in a trillion tiny fragments which can't be assembled; so if you build your stance way off afar on the outer ring of it—is mightily hard to fight your way back in to God.

Clonipin, Wellbutrin, Paxil, —pharmaceutical mental drugs is the evidence of all the problems these kids have—like a disc, smooth side, perfect grooves, turn it over one side is missing, rough, uncut, gibberish. Not well put together.

My time out here is going to be limited—the Lord has told me.

The upward path is so difficult; the pulling away from the old things that will kill you, like sad drug habits & unrequited man-boy love.

Oh, have I told you? 5 of the OGM down here are fighting for their lives, or have recently done so; cancer, and one heart.

Saturday, June 8
When he walked into the doors of Grace the *Amens* were thick.

Defend oh Lord your servant; continue in Your service and increase in Your Holy Spirit while he-she comes to everlasting grace.

A hand snuck over the row; *Peace Senior,* exclaimed a white man, shaking OM's hand.

Sorrow. Sorrow—the earth. Gladness; —in God.

In its limited ways & resources, society, its police and jailers, therapists and lawmakers are trying to deal with subject of child sexual abuse, go about it slightly missing the mark—in punishing 'offenders' makes them turn to virulent hate; some more likely to continue even further up the path—angrily—for revenge. This must not happen.

The light that shines within.

Healing, change.

It has to come up from within the soul.

Have spoken on this subject before, as it pertains to myself, personally. The lines in my books referring to---what is it? A hunger in your soul? The lost childhood, the damaged beginning? Isolation, loneliness, mental illness?

Only speak from my own feelings; the perverse as revenge.

Abandon—a thing set apart.

I know my works will speak to transgenders, transvestites, sex workers, & junkies everywhere—to the iconoclast.

The twisting around of things.

Grace cathedral happens to be one of the cities most loveliest landscapes.

Well I am up here; of course young Junior will not meet me, dragging his heavy black duffel bag plus backpack; and feel vulnerable because of earlier anxiety mixup w/pet food delivery; plus sexual and societal angst.

Re: this man-boy love it is challenging—and abusive to the older person, not just the youth. The older man knows it's a given that his young sex-trade is going to run off w/a woman, or man his own youthful age—and very, very few of these encounters grow into relationships—if that's even what is desired.

Make no peace w/oppression.

So these words trouble me—as some interpret these adventures into the more troubled avenues of society as oppressive.

Here he sat, wrestling w/his demons.

He mulled, how he would write a treatise on the subject: *No prurient material will be included in this missive.*

It is wrong to be in partnership w/oppression; it is wrong to damage another human being. If one sees ones thoughts & feelings are leading down the lesser path one should stop! Turn around!

On the other hand its very good to examine ones inner thoughts & feelings. For instance the mileage I get out of it. –I'm driven to delve deeper.

What is certain it deals w/hurt, pain, disappointment, & is fueled by testosterone driving you wild. In a self-expression of a damaging kind. Damaging to self & 2 others.

Some people, their desires overtake them.

Some people they don't want to know about these things, they prefer naivety. Sensing these passions are unsavory & are associated with evil, and would jeopardize their good standing in society they feign innocence & offer the proscribed answers—but will not get their hands a bit dirty in the matter—and eventually reveal they are passing by on the other side. How they can guide one fallen I'll never know.

The dry thirst in the mouth, a honger in the loins, fire—red, destruction on the mind---coupled w/powerful images, photographs which are illegal.

Dominance.

After all these years I'd hopped on that first merry-go-round again.

Well its true people regard, for instance, damaged homeless; people leave them alone—to work out their own problems on their own.

A pigeon soars majestic; grown adult, sturdy wings—round, aerodynamic shape cuts easily thru air like a boat, or jet plane.

Sat out in sun, Coyote. The owner is furiously setting down new rules, casting out her dictums like a Queen from her high throne:

>   Chairs only against wall—not half-way out in sidewalk.

>   If anyone brings a sandwich from somewhere else, even if they buy a coffee here, they can't eat it.

>   75¢ for water.

Comments are:

>   He's a dickhead.

>   I think they're loosing business and gone into tailspin over it—and he's reacting to that—by going crazy.

No young boy trade.

Heard gossip that a wealthy trick is paying our dear Joe much less then other boys on whom he spends $100, or $150 on them for very simple stuff—a quick suck off. —Because he knows Joe is desperate and will accept it.

Did I tell you a while back a certain personage was mad because Grace Art Works was suppose to hang red banners from the lofty ceiling of the cathedral—to match the green ones already hung. They had worn their best red garments that Sunday to match, but there was no red banners, so they were quite pissed.

PM
Nada.

Fucked up morning this AM—got late to church service because of snafu w/PAWS cat/parrot food delivery. Just as well forgo the delivery, and did not stand up young Junior, as he was not there.

Sunday, June 9
A whole tradition of Mary Magdalene forms in the East, which we don't have in the West.

There is certain amount of respect for Mary Magdalene as the prostitute which; we don't have in the West.

Apostle—one who is sent. From the Greek postas—which gives us the postal service.

Mary Mag is witness of the resurrection.

She was at the crucifixion.

She is in the cannon—the cannon is material, which is considered orthodox.

Mary Mag is not just the perpetual sinner but a follower; just like the male disciples.

She hung out w/them.

Pedagogues—teacher. People would follow. Teacher—those seeking to have a good life would follow a teacher.

Communities gather round certain apostles.

324-325 AD, Constantine brings Christianity to Rome thru the council of Nicia.

Where does your authority come from?

110

Christian community --papyrus hand written scrolls were expensive; a rich church might have 3 gospels and the gospel of Thomas & other stuff.

A poor church might have only one scroll.

These most oft-used scrolls were spoken about constantly.

This siphoned down into cannon.

First six pages of this gospel of Mary are missing.

And before this—no visual depiction of the story; it is mostly text and oral.

Oral traditions, legends.

1250 legends of Mary Mag. Mary Mag—the Super Apostle.

410-476 Roman Empire falls, after repeated attacks on Constantine's capitol.

Like edicts, law courts, structures, are being held by the church so the position of the bishop of Rome, inside this structure, later went on to become the pope.

Plagues, famines, wars, all across Europe. People are looking for something to lift them up.

1400 cultural revelation towards modernizing, come out of the Dark Ages which was plagued by vandals, highway men who made a living robbing pilgrims on the road to worship @ holy shrines; so it was hard to travel, the light of learning could not shine, city doors were locked for defense. It was hard to share knowledge.

Mary the aesthetic.

Mary, caught on the sword of controversy.

Mary was from a wealthy family in Magdala. She was a party girl who led a free headstrong life.

Modern day 2014, the church is no longer a positive force in our lives.

Power, intelligence; the soul's high place. Earth is a dark place where demons roam; there is no security—.

The soul ascends thru different levels, and at each it is interrogated by higher powers there.

Church.

Voice of the reverend calls thru the artificial sound tower, surprising him.

Venti sancta spiritu.

> Don't be afraid to touch the dead things & see them live.
> --Rev Dean Jane Shaw

Surprising sermon from Jane Shaw—which I believe in.

Many leave the service without taking communion—huge gothic doors open, cold air races in, as they depart.

We here inside prefer the warmth.

Bless the Lord(ess) my spirit and bless Your Holy Name, Who leads us into life.

Outside, top of hill, where wind whips. The cathedral looms in distance.

The poor old man, so poor & had no $ money but the streets never fail to surprise us. He looked down—there was a large wrapped package—a sandwich he thought—but upon approaching & giving the package a THWACK w/his cane—found it to be a solid chunk of cheese—as heavy as cement! Food! A $15 cheese! A gourmet cheese! Yahooo!!!!!

Street Food. Title for a book?

Giant cheeses.

PM
I had a bar life. Did I tell you? From age 15 until my 40's was in the bars every single night. The taverns were my home—for about 25 years.

Monday, June 10, 12-NOON
FS office on phone, am mailing in my shit. All Will Be Well!

Saw woman known from the old BABYLON FALLING bookstore; no job; she has been out of work since February. Little food, frantic about rent—steals toilet paper from a large hotel nearby. She is 2 years shy of Social Security. But thank God, that's not a long time.

That theatre on my block which had opened about 6 years ago—who I gave them my play to look over, w/self addressed, stamped, envelope, to return—which they never returned nor commented on—is closing. Truck bed stacked w/theatre seats. Heavy-duty stage lights. It is going. FOR RENT sign on it.

Today was a bit frantic. Got to Coyote, and the owner had ordered the nice barrista lady to PU all the customer's chairs & take them back indoors. Its crazy. Sun shining, wind blowing, ambulances wailing, rent boys cruising by; OGM sparse in attendance, chairs disappearing.

Owner (to bariesta):

> Take in all the chairs against the wall.

> Suppose there's customers sitting in them?

> Tell them to pick up their drinks and go over to the parklett!

Little Junior showed up, crazy acting, but accompanied by the kind social worker who tries to show him love. I too show him love & attention. But not cash.

As we walked towards the corner—him following Olde Pervert who is paying $35 to suck his dick—we came upon an Asian man politely poking in trash for cans, but young Junior who is evidently high on something also decided to poke into trash and dug around in it, pawing frantically like a dog, and found a box which he will soon loose I'm sure. Meanwhile, he was overtaken by a stocky older dark-in-complexion black drug dealer. Junior has nerve enough to turn around and ask me: *Say can you loan me $10?* For what? Drugs!

He's going to turn a date—and use some of the money for drugs. Wonder if he'll show up. Am going to bring him an artist board I found, w/2 scrap pieces of canvas from my remnants.

PM
Oh did I tell you once Junior & I both needed to go to the toilet, and its questionable if the management will let young Junior—apparently homeless— use their facilities:

> Red: if they won't let you in, I'll go in first and you go in around the block & go in the back door & I'll let you in.

> Junior: Yeah, then we can shake each other off too.

Working towards a better, more pleasant heart.

Tuesday, June 11
By the side of the road.

Back home waiting for bro Aaron @ 7PM, din.

Fun w/Aaron, discussed modern ideas. The new government must be representative of all people. Our nation, the USA more commonly known to day as the U$A—was founded as a republic—and a Democracy, by the Founding *Fathers*. This idea of democracy—all men are created equal was revolutionary. However, as history has proved, it fell short:

> Women were not considered
> Black slaves were not considered human

114

Here is the story about young Junior:

Red: I walked w/Junior down the block. He was going to visit Jolly
Olde for a date--$30. We crossed the street, and came upon an
Asian gentlemen politely fishing in a garbage can for cans & bottles
w/a metal stick. Seeing the recycler, Junior promptly ran over and
himself began fishing in the trash. Actually more like pawing into it
wildly like a dog. It became obvious it was a paper-recycling bin.
He produced a medium size cardboard box, then began fishing thru
the papers, gathering as many as he could.

Growing tired of this seemingly wasted effort, I proceeded down to
the other end of the block, telling him: *I'll wait for you down there.*
Where upon I did so and seated myself on a fire hydrant to wait.
As I sat I noticed a blax man of dark complexion wearing a red
jersey, he was medium height, and a thick build. He looked @ me,
then looked away. In a while young Junior came down the street @
a subdued gait, carrying his small pack, some clothes given to him
by the kind ministrations of the Youth Center—which xx shouldn't
do, as Junior's on SOS. (Suspension of Services.) Also he had the
cardboard box, which was full of papers.

While we stood talking, the blax man came over to young Junior
ignoring me, and the two talked—then Junior turns to me & asks:
Hey man can I borrow $10?

Of course I replied no. At that point without another word the two
proceed on down the street toward Olde Jolly's shop, without even
a goodby from Junior, alltho the hustling blax man did cast back
one wary look @ me.

Olde Jolly:

Junior came by w/a black man and met me in my doorway. My
next door neighbor sensing trouble came up and asked if I was OK.
At this point the blax man left, and I let Junior in. Instead of turn
the date he sat there and spilled out all these papers all over the
floor and began going thru them. He sorted over those papers for 3
hours! He didn't do anything! We had no date! But I gave him the
$30 I'd promised him, and finally got him to leave by telling him my
security system was about to go off @ 8pm! The first time I had him

115

it was so nice, we laid in the bed naked together, it was so sweet; but never again! Not after last night!

PM

     She found her identity,
drunk on Gin.
Swaggering Juvenile, act the fool.
Jailbait, she was kicked out of Chicago's
   only dyke gay bar.
& by time she turned 18
Vicesquad had busted the rest.
As raids persecuted us.
   Desperate, she sought lovers
   in hustling bars, among alcoholic
   prostitute women.
Drunk, she fights. Her nights on skidrow;
   her misfit youth among ruined faces.
--The Magician (COLLECTED POETRY, VOL. 2)

All this crazy shit w/loosing then gaining back my stupid shitly Food Stamps, medical coverage etc, has shown me the devils great preoccupations.

Their class, Priest Jude mentioned how the soul ascends from earth thru many layers of heaven maybe like kindergarten heaven, then grade 1 thru 6 grammar school heaven, then high-school heaven, then post-graduate heaven etc., where in each layer of heaven the soul is interrogated w/many spiritual questions having to do with the person's values, earthy deeds etc. On earth are wars, famines, pestilence, and no security of anything. Here on earth demons are free to roam—damaging what ever they can get a hold of.

So a devoted Christian who seeks a higher Christian path on earth, must certainly have to begin cutting ties w/earth—of a material denomination— least they be so tied-up they can't really progress spiritually forward closer to God. In fact the daily paying of bills, balancing budgets, working for bread, are all hurdles in the spiritual seekers path. They discover Karl Marx and landlords and working for too little wages so as to be controlled by other humans, who more clever, that hold their purse strings. So, at some juncture they learn to join w/sister/fellow Christians of like minds, and equal dedication, and begin to live communally so as to be able to sever those materialistic ties.

It is of great value if a band of Christians can live together sharing rents, washing/drying machines, kitchens, food cooking, because if they can function together harmoniously it frees them individually to do works of spirit, and not be tied down, each individually, to a shit job 40 hours per week.

Oh spoke w/bro Aaron about Baz, and the chauffer service—turns out Aaron too had driven chauffer service. The prerequisite is must own your own car. Well, it turns out he too earned very good money—but it wore down his car, eventually the car broke! He never did that job again! Hope this don't happen to China-brother man, because he lives heullafar away, and truly needs a car for self-commute to SF, to anywhere civilized actually!

> I had food and some stuff in my pack. I set it down. Somebody took it.
> --Joe.

To remind you there is no honor among thieves. These homeless will kill, rape, steal, attack, each other. They are messed up and bad humanity. They are worthy of being helped, but don't be misled, they are among the worse of the worst.

Young Junior too, has had all his stuff stolen. The found cellphone I gave him, clothes, his drawings, the sketchbook (given to me) I gave him. All the free shit they gave him @ the youth center. He acts like he don't care. These thieves are the homies he loves so much, other homeless. It is not rich yuppies stealing his shit!

Smoking from basement has been unbearable. If I had nothing to loose I'd get my gun and go down there and kill the bastards.

Have to take the trouble to email the property manager once a damn gain!

Soon will tell you the tale of —Olde Perv: —it took Junior 3 hours—sorting!

Wednesday, June 12
So asked my therapist about young Junior—every time I tell him: *I wish you wouldn't use drugs—its fucking you up. Crank and crack kill people, and so does heroin.* And he responds: *I can't think without it. I'm no good, I'm not my real self without it.* So she told me to ask him:

How does the crank help you think?

What does it do? Does it help you focus?

Does it help you relax?

Does it help you be more creative?

Does it help you feel better about yourself?

Is your mood better?

Are you less socially awkward? Is it easier to be around people?

What a day this has been, what a struggle.

Birds sail thru air like boats.

Marquee letters pried off the face of the theatre—just a dusty outline of where they were—the stupid theatre that did not pay my play any attention is gone.*

Miss Daisy says she's getting out of town on a vacation: *I'm gettin' out of here! Too many problems out here. Hell no I'm not going out of the country! I've never been out of the US!*

A collard green cake. A soul picnic chicken; wings drenched in hot sauce. Mountains of chicken wings.

*--A tranny play, Carnivella, I believe.

118

One of the old 5 coffee shops appears to be on the verge of opening—all modernized. Wonder if their old grey habitués will return there...
--GROWING WISDOM—1

The answer to this question came from Mark; Sculptor, Glazier, who was an aficionado of the joint. *No, none of the old regulars are coming back. They all hate it.* Me & Dr. Sam went there the other nite—all tall stools and counter tops, the type you feel vertigo—like you're falling off of them; no regular chairs.

> He bought a perfectly good coffee shop that was making money, but he had to go and change it around, the way he wanted it. Now nobody wants to go in the place. Why did he have to meddle with it? It's shit.
> --Mark, Glazier

Oh, last nite w/Aaron @ Lories Restaurant, the young artist told me:

> David's leaving. He's leaving town. He's going back to the East Coast, New Jersey, where he's from. He's had it w/San Fran.

PM
Nada.

Thursday, June 13
Well I must say man in basement is interesting, & we are somewhat similar—I called him a troll; maybe he's lying, but he presents a picture of all kinds of people smoking—including the Chinaman @ end of our hallway corner who have lived there forever—could his smoke somehow be making it under my floorboards? According to his report, @ 2AM he sits in the window smoking gales of cigarette smoke.

Saw Joe, handsome, so strong built—a red shirt stretched over his muscular chest; needs a shave. Stupidly asked him how he was doing. ***"OK..."*** Joe answers icily, his swarthy face dripped morbidity:

> **Ok, considering its cold @ night; freezing, and cops harassing you. Moving you along for blocking the sidewalk. & getting ticket**

after ticket. These people move in here and they think an alley is something special, its just a fucken' alley…

Yeah, but they're remodeling all the alleys, and selling expensive condos in the alleys, so the rich yuppies are screaming & complain.

Complaining, there's homeless out in my alley! The fucken' yuppie pussies! The pussies! Its not like we're breaking in their car windows or nothin! We're not doing anything to them!

$40 almost gone. Wait for Grace. Will not worry. Work on my files for $ art.

It was time to go. Music had begun its 2nd go round—3 hours since played the same tune as when he'd first arrived.

PM
So what happened earlier this week, a whole gang of us was sitting in the parklet—re; owners edict that we can't sit on the edge along the building in more then 2 chairs and there was 6 of us. And that day Junior & the Olde Pervert linked up. The next day the whole gang is sitting together, and I recount the tail of how the previous afternoon young Junior went down to the corner and came back highly under the influence of narcotics, and up the street we went together, me towards the Ho's, and him to turn the date, and he dug into the trash looking for identity theft papers—foolishly.

So next day we're all sitting together, sans young Junior, and here come Jolly Olde across the street, and he sits down and recounts the tail of their date they supposedly had that night:

> He comes in and empties out this cardboard box full of papers on the floor and begins sorting thru them and sorts and sorts for 3 hours. I saw him naked for 1 minute when he got up and changed into those new pants and threw the bluejeans full of holes in the trash. He just kept sorting thru those papers. Then I gave him $30 and kicked him out. I paid him but he didn't do a damn thing. Nothing.

I look back over my life—the many groups I associated w. Most were gay/third-sex groups. The originals were straight black/brown groups. Then artist groups---all of these marginalized! I have been an outlaw from day one! By who I am!

Somehow we found each other.

> Yes, you are different.
> And yes, you have something rare.
> Every step I take, every
>   breath I make,
> I am revolutionary.
> I am radical
>   because of what I am.
> --THE MAGICIAN, COLLECTED POEMS

Aurrgh! Just had to go thru WISDOM- 2 notes compiling to make 1st edition, to edit out young Junior's real name, which inadvertently used.

Saw MTF woman I know—Had been talking about a low-cost seniors housing building we passed, and she told me what she knew about it; described their tiny independent units, and I told her what I knew about it, how the staff steals—the cleaning staff.

She tells me she worked all her life w/the objective in mind never to be put @ the mercy of any system: *Honey, no, the jail system, the nursing home system, the government, the welfare system—none of 'em.*

Friday, June 14
It was egregious thing—to put a paten on a human gene! This Utah corporation squatted on the paten rights, which our Supreme Court now overturned! Now the price for use of a genetic test involving that particular gene has dropped dramatically! Our human genes are given to us by Creator, and cannot be patented for exclusive use of any corporation!

Persistence—went to art gallery again, lady was in, but on phone. Her white girl bodyguard this time; again took my card and number.

I am privileged to live in a city where all these great visitors from Washington DC fly in to do fundraising. Security shows in force—a battalion of police officers. One in the crowd of us waiting for the motorcade to pass exclaims: *all that for Joe Biden?* Guard 2nd in command of our nation.

Motorcycle cops blue uniforms zip past @ huge rate of speed then blax shiny SUV vans carrying the politicians raced by --2nd in command of our nation his finger on the nuclear weapons trigger fire if the President was disabled.

More blue unformed motorcycle cops gunned past then the last motorcycle cop honked horn on his bike loudly —and the whole parade closed into itself, zooming up the street—and the intersection returned to normal, the procession sped away into the distance, vanished.

As the OM sat on one of his ledges he sniffed the scent of passing humans—mostly strong men's cologne. A fleet of pink moustaches sail past, transporting affluent people.

He barely had had enough to pay for his dinner:

> *cheese,*
> *beans,*
> *corn.*

> *$4.89*

When a dingy blax homeless shuffled by politely asked: *can you buy me some dinner pulese?* Wondered if/when this homeless had spent his true dinner money previously on crack or liquor.

It got cold, almost unbelievably cold @ night; yet, almost unbearably hot during the day.

PM
There some things money will not buy. No amount of money. A rich man's son is killing himself w/use of drugs and will not stop. The rich man pays for one treatment after another, and nothing will

prevent his son from drug use. The treatment seems to work, the family has high hopes, tens of thousands of dollars are spent—but the son has tricked them for once again he resumes his addiction. No amount of money will stop it. Something's money won't buy, only Spirit. There are prices that can be paid in spirit, by Spirit, thru Spirit—the Spirit of the Eternal has been courted by humankind for eons. For fertility, crops, healing; things prayed for, supplicated for, fasted for, asked for, and sometimes answered.

Saturday, June 15
Thank God! My Grace check has come!

I'm almost there; sez Jasmin—irate. Minutes pass— no Jasmin. 15 minutes later she is waiting outside; & me no coat, it is cold.

Um um um; so good. He ate w/fork, spoon, chopsticks—and finally w/his hands. Chinese barbeque.

Saw Junior. Loaned him a sketchbook to draw in—and he must give it back.

Junior had a battle w/Cosmo, they yelled @ each other.

This is not good.

I'm gonna kill that Cosmo, Junior said.

Show tunes play outside. After all the excitement the Old Man sat in the cold in his coat, waiting for arrival of Baz.

Junior sat & drew in his book awhile.

Very good talk w/Donna Marchusa, artist: *You must do your passion! Every night you must paint!* She declares. Donna lectured us on the importance of art.

Donna talked about serendipitous events. How the universe opens things up to show us—and noone else sees it but us, and thru this we grow or are rewarded.

123

Now its freezing to death. All tables & chairs are still out—every single one, whereas 2 days in the hot blazing sun, all the tables & chairs against the café wall were gone, and most had vanished out here in the parklet.

This makes absolutely no business sense.

Every table, every chair—blue, green, all colors of tables, and a setting of 4 chairs each around each one and the benches! Every chair & table in the house still sitting outside here in the cold—empty.

Calling upon the Eternal.

Adonai, Shema, Eloheim, El, Jehovah: *My Name is many Names.* Names, utterances.

PM
Bro Baz wined & dined this old guy—later @ the culmination of the evening he said something—which was redolent of what Donna Marcusa, Artist, had said earlier, like hers I will try to remember/paraphrase his:

> Its cosmic elements, which have brought us all here together in this place, San Francisco. In my 2 years in America I've lived, grown; grown so much dude, can you see me in Malaysia, afraid of the police—the police might murder me--because they don't understand, we T don't have any rights.

There go God's children. The unknown, unloved, uncared for, unwanted. Straggling down street; many burdens, packages, backpacks.

Joe came down the alley, looking fine, powerful built, wearing black trousers shirt, handsome; accompanying a slim used girl, but on closer sight saw a 5 o'clock shadow of a man's beard begun on her face— it's a more or less unsuccessful passing T girl.

A police van raced down Polk, descending towards the jail. BANG, CRASH loud fists/ feet punched again metal walls of van as prisoner inside is freaking out.

Police racing to get the prisoner out of sight/hearing of the public.

Big fat pigeons sail in the sky back towards their sun warm pigeon-heated homes—ledges of roofs; windowsills.

YOU SEE! Title book?

Sunday, June 16
Out. The Sabbath. No classes.

Did I tell you Cosmo said/did something funny the other day—him & Joe were seated @ Coyote, argument ensued, Joe w/his quiet barely audible voice, the older man, animated, strong, loud voice; Cosmo got up & walked over to a gold cauldron & leaned there to get away. Somebody commented how they were separate, and he said: --*oh, we're together, all Joe needs is my wallet anyway, not me, he don't need me to sit w/him, just put my wallet right there in the other chair, and he'll do just fine.*

One more time we got together, Annie spoke about compassion—acceptance of one another.

I'm tired I'm old. I've tried to get close to humanity as I can. I did not stand in the circle @ the worship service but sat up in the pews.

YOU ARE HERE, THAT IS ENOUGH.

Halleluiah!

Snap! Tourists photograph the great cathedral from the top of her gothic spire, the apex of her 3 stories long stained glass windows, to the well-worn pews; to the gold emblazoned kyros set in the marble floor.

SNAP! SNAP! Invasive. The service progresses.

Annie told a funny joke:

> There was this roach-eating contest in Florida. All these people, young people, had a roach-eating contest—the person who could

125

eat the most roaches would win. So this man ate 30 roaches—and he died.

Yeah, from all the pesticides inside those roaches.

Roaches have every virus, germ, disease, and pesticides---that's all they eat.

What was the prize he won for eating all those roaches?

The prize you won was a snake.

Ha ha ha, so there is a contest to see who can eat the most roaches—and the winner gets a snake! How funny. Ugh.

PM
TV program about genealogy—discovered slave facts. Many slaves were freed by their masters. A will might declare upon the master's death their slaves be given freedom. Some then might make their way North, fearing being recaptured by unscrupulous whites who might catch them, tear up their free papers and haul them back into slavery. So to make one's way to the free states North, was to greatly lessen the chance of recapture.

A horrible tale was told of a man given such freedom; who then went & purchased all his own children and declared them free. The family made their way North and settled in free state of Ohio—right across the Ohio River, which divided Ohio from the slave state of Kentucky. Across this river black slaves, and white men could see them from the opposite shore. About a year later during the night some white men rowed across the Ohio, broke down the man's door and kidnapped all his young children, throwing them into gunny sacks and took them back across the Ohio River, selling them into slavery again to several masters.

The intrepid black free man took his case to the US Court—and was granted 4 of his children back from the slave holding state of Kentucky, but the slave holding state of Virginia—bastion of slavery— would not give him custody of his other 4 children; slaves they remained until the Emancipation Proclamation and Civil War freed all the slaves, a decade later.

126

This is most horrific & horrible of worlds & this is because it allows such horror to remain inside of itself—without a care. Now heaven is a beautiful world—a wonderful world....

Monday, June 17
The former Persian coffee shop is closed again today--under its new owner. Bad location, bad spot. Bad fung shui.

Tall white man very nice but steps, one step ahead of Transman; boy is he furious. Waits only a minute, then it is his turn. Purchasing small coffee @ Coyote.

Sitting facing direction street; sun brilliant but soon to go.

Joe came by so dejected; but skin bronzed & handsome.

Coyote, saw Joe, sitting fierce; deep bronzed street-dwellers skin.

Olde made date w/him for tomorrow, $40. Joe seemed pleased, and suddenly more light-hearted.

Me no money until August.

Next free $40 I get must OCR! AC 2, or PASSAGE-4.

Cigarette went flying across street. Half smoked. Eagle eyed, Joe ran between traffic; his sturdy gait, leaned over somewhat Nethanderthal manner—of one who carries very heavy packages unceasing.

Darts thru traffic across street soon returns puffing it in his lips.

PM
Nada.

Tuesday, June 18
Cell phone cameras out, aimed @ sky—perfectly round rainbow high up in the heavens; yellow, red purple, white haze. One of the extraordinary halo-rainbows which appears every 5 years or so.

When he got out there was only the barest light circle of the halo remaining, white, like smoke & sun blazing shone thru it, blinding to the eye.

PM
Nada.

Wednesday, June 19
March about on errands. Ran into the debonair photog Thai Shaun Roberts. He bought me some WallGrims salami, ham, cheese, bananas.

When he got to the café, there was a full house seated in the parklet. The handsome Cosmo, young Junior cuddled to one side, the strong, sun bronzed Joe, the woman w/dog, another older trick, and the very handsome and nice barkeep from down the way. So much candy, so little time!

You go first-then you—then XXX. Little Junior is turning a date w/*All* of them.

Police rode around, clean-cut, short hair; scooping the street.

So much action.

Everybody is collateral. Everybody, even the stupid.

An ultra upscale yup goes past; wallet full of necessary credit cards, and folding green money, $100 bills. So much money.

In this city disco music beats! Swoon singers, breathy, so much in need.

Work it! Work it!

PM
Such a difficult world—harming the weakest, dunning me w/letters, this is shit. This system is broke.

Joe talks about racism in jail:

It's almost all black. There was only 2 of us white guys in jail; I couldn't use the phone, I couldn't use the computer, I couldn't take a shower. I couldn't get into use the weights in the weight area. It sucks.

See by my notes the notation OGM. Should describe this bunch more. Are a total of 8 of them—counting all stragglers who only appear occasionally, and aged from 50 to 95.

Red thought, re: the two rent boy: *He is beyond my reach.*

But not Mine. Says the Lord(ess).

Thursday, June 20

Read the scriptures—when I climb up to the high podium, towering above the congregation; from the pulpit of the gothic cathedral I got into the scripture, then came back out w/all of it!

So little Junior got fucked by 3 guys last afternoon—not penetrative sex; valiantly he jacked his big meat off—on crack, so he couldn't cum.

The older men gave little Junior Viagra, and he had an immense hard on—which wouldn't go away. One of the guys left his joy juice on the computer. So Junior watches porn, jerking off frantically trying to get his nut, got the mouse all greasy, and the computer keyboard and the table, even the screen, and the arms on the computer chair all greasy w/joy juice before he finally succeeded in cuming.

It has not been a good life. Friends lost. Lovers broken apart. In the past we had to hide. If we were not able to hide we faced danger to the death.

Have you ever noticed how some people you encounter you may hate, loath, can't stand, think: *ICK!* towards them --& most of them can be your same gender, race, age…

Beautiful rainbow flag unfurls on Market Street—our gay Day Parade next Sunday. Deep bright blue, purple; lavish crimson reds.

Sitting w/gay guys in sleepy Castro, ate a bit of lunch. Got cruised by older gentleman.

Junior's case worker was there in her home away from home--
Coyote: *How can you not like them, their so cute, they're just kids.*
To which the male caseworker said: *yeah, but if you see them in a gang they're not so cute.*

Yea; because their empowered w/each other—and they wind up spending their lives in jail over that.

PM
Nada.

A lot of people don't see, they come here, straights, women, families w/kids, sit, politely having their expensive lunch in this outdoor cafe—they don't see the scene, which transpires just below –in subtext; young hustlers, older men looking for them, down here…

All speak of young Junior's big cock: *He has a big cock.* And all want that meat.

Friday, June 21
Street woman screams @ man holding shopping bag: SET THAT DOWN HERE! SET IT DOWN BITCH!

On sidewalk, the terrible homeless.

We all walk; carry our burdens.

Got to Coyote; 2 OGM just leaving. Speaking of health problems, 70% of us are having issues—big ones. (Cancer, Heart, Diabetes.)

Must say my head was all in a whirl w/this man-boy sex stuff (over 18, over 22 in fact) & cute young man nestled next to me—surrounded by his back packs and gloomy young proud ego know-it-all—defeating his purpose: *I don't want to be inside! I want to be outside!* Where he sleeps, and gets robbed of his valuables: dope, cell phone, and cash. And Penny is in my heart--& pray she will eat, plus give her treatment tonight.

There is a lot of material in here in this coastal city.

The drama is spreading privately so now after yesterdays fast & wild outdoor party is no one—but me & my infernal NOTES describing the skeleton of my times--the structure— & which provides me money—

I was always a lonely child.

An old trick white hair drives past in a fancy expensive SUV, w/ picture of the Virgin Mary on his dashboard—in full color, 8"x12" laminated—in floral color in a lovely golden frame, dressed in a bridal gown.

Furious copulation, foam splaying under this picture of the Virgin Mother of our Lord(ess) on his knees in painful position penance…

Your dark thoughts will be wiped away. Your pure ones remain.

I am covered by the Blood of Jesus Christ & my sins forgiven me.

We've got to pick the dirt up---says the Gardener, w/a supreme irony.

The Gardener is furiously gardening… planting flowers before sunset.

A dumb homeless man pushes his shopping cart full of stale found food, recyclables—he is low IQ—what happens to these—w/all this lack of training programs—?

Flowers bloom in the golden cauldrons, pink, white, yellow, lavender; bloom in abundance—their green stalks grown so high they are taking over the sidewalk—patrons can't see each other around them.

The lowest act is to provide drugs for sex—you get more that way. More bang for the buck. You can get the drugs, and its cheaper then paying sex for it—it is so low. Down the street @ Diva's you would see this all the time, men, mostly Hispanic workers, come in talk to a girl, they offer her drugs for sex and out they go together, like lovers. He will get his cock sucked, his balls worked over.

The Great Chair Removal has begun for the afternoon—its only 3:30.

Saw young man XX walk by—he is an employee in the Dirty Bookstore—

Patrons come out of café—holding plates of food, drinks—but can find no tables, chairs in this outdoor café—part of its charm—so they retreat indoors.

A young woman obviously hooker self-composed crosses one leg over the other; she sports high high leopard pattern shoes, very elegant, Asiatic. Mixed race?

She balances back on points of the ultra high heels--- rolls a cigarette, runs flame over it--to seal it. Marijuana—then lights a real cigarette.

Searching thru her phone. No doubt for dates.

Material goods come to them so fast on the streets; cellphones, shoes, clothes, leather coats, jewelry, --& so soon lost.

1 block down is stark contrast to this hi-fashion hooker; a degraded human being squats between 2-parked cars. Naked ass down to the gutter; see their naked legs, reaches between their bare thighs w/toilet paper—taking a shit. 5pm, daylit.

Nowhere to use the toilet in San Francisco.

> Nowhere to sing.
> Nowhere to dance.
> Nowhere to do art,
> in San Francisco.
> --Popular refrain, 1990's

This predatory blax streetman running a donation scram w/a laminated book he carries, mean; he approached Transman and a poor street woman w/mental illness, w/her dog. Transman politely told him he was not interested, but he persisted, turning his attention to the meek young woman. He kept talking & talking @ her, finally Transman asserted himself saying:

132

Why don't you leave her alone; I don't think she's interested!

Well let her tell me that!

Frankly sir, I mean no offense, but I think she's afraid of you, and she's too afraid to say no to you!

The man was verging on rage, but it was probably fear of the police, which made him back down.

The hustler tried to shake Transman's hand, but he shook his head and would not shake his hand, but instead used the Asian bow, his hands clasped together in prayer. This way you can appear friendly, but not trust your hand to a stranger who might be psychotic, & not let go of your hand!

The frail woman had begun to dig into her purse for coins—but Transman had run the fool off. Later he asked her: *did you want to talk to that guy?* And she responds, dreamy-voiced: *I don't know...*

This woman suffers from severe psychotic disorders, also she is extremely poor, & lucky to be housed. She is bi-polar.

Then the Lord(ess) spoke to him saying, loudly to his spiritual ear: *Thank You!*

I spoke to one of the younger OGM about the incident, and he gave a strange response, regarding the girl: *They want equal; rights, let them stand up for themselves.*

Talked about this matter w/Annie:

What was your intention? I think that is what matters.

I was trying to protect the young woman.

PM

So much hatred is directed at homosexuality. Their reasoning is logical to the enemy. But when I see a big 6 foot tall, 150-pound sissy prancing around in nylons and a mini-skirt and lipstick, his

133

nose in the air, I know it is not his clothing that's a sin, the sin is that he is robbed of his heart.
--ALEXANDER D'ORO Circa 1975

God says S/He is going to show me what God wants me to do for Her-Him, --will delineate it—I agree w/it. I just follow the plan.

The church; sexism; needs centuries worth—of undoing.

Saturday, June 22
Day. Some of the high upscale people w/riches go past—some of the murky souls of homeless in dark stained clothes shuffle along gutters search for cigarette butts---

Sitting in Coyote.

All work you do holistically.

When the human safety net breaks down someone will fall thru.

The OM had w/him now a little party of the downtrodden. W/bags & dogs they were frowned upon by the Owner, however he'd made sure to provide them each w/a placeholder, and they found a table & spread out along the length of one half.

We sat inside Coyote, w/a $2 cookie on a plate, & 2 coffees. A woman & her nice dog, a youth, & him. A little art drawing class. Later Transman went outside, his face to the sun.

The erotic force is something never tell who it will flow thru—like chi—nor whom you might become attached to... Mother Nature has her ways...

We parade a few moments on this stage.

I guess it takes a while to uncurl; to unwind from some problems—the damage done to you in youth—years of free floating thru bars & streets & alcohol & drugs; wandering thru your mind—until some kind of better impulse—encourages you upward—to climb out of yourself, to climb out of your pain— & live in reality again.

134

So here we sit—the woman is 20 years older then the youth & 30 years younger then the OM. The OM is 45 years older then the youth.

The white folks—these genetic new breeds on the human chain.

Back outside in the sun with lady w/dog, now gone—Junior still inside w/his backpacks spilled w/miscellaneous articles all over the table.

So the OM spent very pleasant day in the sun.

Another table full of upscale yups drunks— whole table of glasses, plates, sophisticated longstem wine glasses; they fall to the ground: CRASH!

Pigeon hi-step struts on red feet.

Life.

PM
A passel of gals poses outside men's sex club in costume, ultra high heels; one woman down on her knees, pantomiming giving the other woman head. One of her sisters, the 4th woman photographs them: SNAP SNAP!

Into the men's sex club the go.

Sodom & Gomorrah!

Dr Sam calls, we drive to coffee/Mel's diner. It's a super moon tonight. Moon closest to earth then it will be for a year. Out again @ Mel's diner w/Dr. —Late nite scrambled egg w/cheese & bacon. Told me:

> There's a bunch of people have gotten together, they are raising funds, charging $50 a ticket, to win a lottery, for two people, for those who want to be on a spaceship to Mars—and settle on Mars in a geodesic dome. They will create their own oxygen; grow their own food inside this dome. Only one thing. It's a one way TX.

So of course we debated on what kind of mind could sustain a 3-year trip to the planet Mars in a space capsule, then live out their life on a planet w/no other people around. And no possible return route home. We both agreed one or both of the people needed to be neutered; they could not have children there. It would be an unbearable fate to resign that child to.

When the two exited, the wind was rushing strong, hard, & the sky thick w/fog. Rainy moisture in the air. The dark night. Streets deserted.

Sunday, June 23
One of the problems w/healing is the healer-person believing healing is generated within *themselves*, and passed into the sick person to be healed. This is not true. Healing is generated by *God*; passed to the healer, who then passes it into the sick person, so they can be healed.

We are empty creatures, given vitality for our own personal robust existence. When we ask for the gift of healing it is given, *thru us*, to give to others—given from where? From GOD THE ETERNAL!

Bells in campanile don't ring—no point waiting for them to signal service is about to begin.

Spoke w/older—knowledgeable parishioner/volunteer @ Grace— heard the story of the infamous Bishop Pike who was noted for his esoteric spiritual-searching.

> The bishop was @ pulpit preparing to deliver his sermon for a diocesan commemorative annual event--when the call came into the Vestry:
>
> *This is the NYPD* (New York Police Department). *Your son has been found dead, gunshot to the head, self inflected. What shall we do w/the body?*
>
> The son couldn't live w/the fact he was gay—back in those bigoted times of the 1960's.

The bishop then turned to the occult, consulting spirits, life after death, mediums, the study of karma, and other current fads of the wild hippy 1960's. All the while retaining his high position in the far more orthodox Christian Episcopalian church. It was this that gave him the strange reputation which trickled out into the public, even down to the atheistic drinkers & poolshooters in the gay bar Wild Side West, where young pre-Transman shot pool and partied on 25-cents for Coca Cola in a glass mug every night of the week—for his social life.

The rumor had it, further, that the good Bishop had gone to the Middle East in his spiritual pursuits to seek the afterlife and find his dead son, so rudely snatched away from him—and in his seeking, wandering, got lost in the desert and was never heard from again.

Well actually it was more simple:

> Shortly after his son's death Bishop Pike and his 3rd wife went on a trip to Israel. They were driving along the highway when the car ran out of gas. The sun in the desert was baking 130%. Full of confidence Pike left his wife in the car, and headed off into the desert to get help—the 70-year old Pike was uncovered, in a scorching desert w/no shade, nor water. Wisely the wife got out of the car, opened the door, and huddled under it in the patch of shade made by the vehicle and focused on her survival.

> A few hours later the Israeli police force came driving along in a jeep. They rescued the wife and went out searching for the bishop. His body was recovered a few days later.

Of course the child Junior is not here, nor his friend the young woman w/dog.

My God this life is difficult. Went into the courtyard before the 6 o'clock. Gazed @ the face of gray granite 3rd story gothic peeked windows. Cold wind blows. Fountain gushers cold water. The crippled woman, insane, bent almost double, shuffles silently away. Such torture until life ends.

3-of us trans here in the service. 1, another brother am not sure of. Also one congregant hi yella, I believe (Black). *Maybe.* —Doubt is due to the fact that these white girls have gone to curling their hair, bronzing their skin under sun lamps and poofing out their lips w/plastic surgery, so they looks like a sista. We have such secret lives.

Did I mention, my eye has developed a twitch, because of stress. About my Penny cat, and little Junior; also older dark-haired Joe. — Drug addict.

Spiritual insight revealed Joe, Junior, and the lady w/the dog are all spiritually bound. They are bound by the darker forces, and every day of their lives are continuing to be bound tighter—unless they can break loose and seek the Highest Power—the Eternal—led thru Jesus Christ, and venture further along the road.

A triad of dikes walks past outside Laundromat window; black leather. This is Gay Pride week. A very femmy gay Asian man flounces out w/designer bag of fresh clothes.

Dollar by dollar the shopkeepers earn their living. Till the end of time.

Was witness @ table when little Junior reached into one of his voluminous backpacks, picked out a bottle of blue substance and poured some into his mouth & promptly spit it out:

> UUUGGGHGHHHHHHAAAAAHHH!

The bottle was nailpolish remover.

> **JUNIOR DON'T DRINK ANY MORE! IT'S NAILPOLISH REMOVER!**
>
> *I THOUGHT IT WAS MOUTH WASH!*
>
> **RINSE OUT YOUR MOUTH!**
>
> **IT LOOKS LIKE MOUTHWASH!**

Junior exclaimed holding the open plastic bottle of green liquid.

SPIT IT OUT! SPIT IT OUT! We all cried; several, including Transman thrust glasses of water @ him.

    RINSE OUT YOUR MOUTH AND SPIT IT OUT! DON'T SWALLOW IT!

PM

There is a lot of dirty dirt up here @ Grace—the wise ones know, — these who have dedicated their church life to serving here in the Cathedral— that this is a human condition. It is not endemic to Grace. And oblivious to it, they plunge on ahead in their church service, undaunted, serving to the end to keep her noble ship floating, and endowing her w/their financial wills upon their demise. Grace is not the first church I attended after my quarter-century of atheism, and I learned in that other church the wickedness, gossip, backbiting, jockeying for positions and all the shit. Just as I had first-hand knowledge of the hypocrisy, child-molestation, of my first, original church. So it comes as no surprise to see the same thing in other churches, and synagogues.

The church was a festival of hope that evening the OM went about lighting candles for his Penny, praying underneath the icon of *Jesus As Teacher*, against the asp beside the Gold Crucifix, and requesting of several priests & some parishioners for prayers for someone, and when they all asked: *what is the person's name?* He told them: *Penny.* And as usual cast up his regular prayer for her, and for several cases he was working on—namingly young Junior, and Joe, and others. So he had gone all around the cathedral like a big festival grounds speaking to Jesus here and there, as one does when one visits amusement booths, — lighting flames, praying and telling his needs.

This is a way to utilize your church—prayers en mass. They are supposed to work and be most powerful.

I remember, I was just sitting in church—by the asp—during the service, just as we began to line up for Communion—the Spirit of Jesus Christ came to me, and hung on for about 20 minutes, while the lines of people circled up to receive the Host, Blood, me among them, then faded after I'd returned to my seat and the finishing of the service. I had not asked anything of God that particular day, Jesus

139

just came in. I had dedicated my life to God over and over, and over and over and over and over and over and had asked for the spiritual gift of healing before. So this coming to me was a prayer of quite a while back, now answered.

Corinthians was tonite's scripture and it told of Jesus casting the legion—demons— out of the wildly tormented insane man who dwelt naked among the tombs. They told Jesus: *We are many*. Imagine the horror of that sufferer, possessed by all those devils. Jesus with all power healed the man; he cast the man's demons into a herd of swine who then plunged into the sea.

Jude Harmon's sermon went on to speak about, how the people of the town were terrified at this working of a miracle, and actually begged Jesus to leave their town—to leave them alone! Can you imagine! Many sufferers lived in this town plagued by myriad human conditions of the human body and mind, which Jesus could easily have solved, but the town's people were so terrified they just wanted him to leave!

Any healer or any other gifted by the divine must go into it knowing their life will be forever changed. They will no longer be able to live as an anonymous simple person, overlooked by the majority of the world.

Are you ready for it?

YES!

While he had been typing the Lord(ess) had overtaken him just a bit, so he was a tad drowsy, and the Lord(ess) brought remembrance to mind, of how Jesus had come to him—so it would be like this Jesus would come back—with instructions, information.

The healing would be done within a body of like-minded congregants, who were praying (if 2 or more are gathered together in My Name), it would be accompanied by teaching. And instruction, as God would not have us mystified. The evidence, in scriptures, would be analyzed, spoken of, the truth revealed to the masses of people who have remained ignorant—because of not wanting to take the time to

140

search for the truth—in so many texts where scripture is analyzed printed published free, and given to us; available!

Red Jordan Arobateau
Friday, July 4, 2013
9PM, Pacific Standard Time
San Francisco, CA